Europe
1870-1914

Edited by

Peter Catterall

and

Richard Vinen

Heinemann

HISTORY BRIEFINGS

Heinemann Educational
a division of Heinemann Publishers (Oxford) Ltd.
Halley Court, Jordan Hill, Oxford OX2 8EJ

OXFORD   LONDON   EDINBURGH
MELBOURNE   MADRID   ATHENS
BOLOGNA   PARIS   SYDNEY
AUCKLAND   SINGAPORE   TOKYO
IBADAN   NAIROBI   HARARE
GABORONE   PORTSMOUTH NH (USA)

First published 1994

British Library Cataloguing in Publication Data

A catalogue record for this book is available from the British Library

ISBN 0 435 31004 6

98 97 96 95 94
10 9 8 7 6 5 4 3 2 1

Typeset by CentraCet Ltd, Cambridge

Printed in Great Britain by Clay Ltd, St Ives plc.

Front cover: *Il Quarto Stato* by Giuseppe Pelliza da Volpedo (Civica
Galleria d'Arte Moderno, Milan)

Acknowledgements

Heinemann and the ICBH wish to thank all the contributors who
have given permission for their work to be published in this book.

Thanks are also due to Philip Allan (Publishers) Ltd for permission
to print articles which originally appeared in the *Modern History
Review*.

Introduction

It is no accident that science fiction should have begun to be widely written and read during the closing years of the nineteenth century. Authors such as Jules Verne and H.G. Wells looked to a world that was to be transformed by the use of technology. Such works appealed to readers who were already beginning to see how their own lives might be transformed by devices such as the railway, the motor car, and the telegraph. Many of these technologies had been known about for many years, but they had not been applied on a scale that was wide enough to change the lives of ordinary people. Some technological developments of the late nineteenth century were comparatively unexciting compared to those (jet engines, atom bombs, television) which would transform the later part of the twentieth century, but the very fact that a man without specialist education might understand the workings of the internal combustion engine in a way that he could never understand, say, nuclear fission contributed to the enthusiasm with which technological change was followed.

Industrial production was transformed during what some historians have labelled 'the second industrial revolution'. Advances in chemistry (such as the Bessemer process for making steel) opened up new industries. This industrial progress had two sorts of consequences. Firstly, it changed relations between the classes. It was widely believed that the industrial concentration which occurred in the late nineteenth century would be accompanied by an intensification of class struggle as large numbers of utterly dispossessed proletarians confronted a tiny plutocracy of enormously rich industrialists. Whether or not this happened is open to debate, but it is certainly true that increasing numbers of people worked in industry and that production was increasingly concentrated in large units. These developments made it easier to organise the working class. Socialist parties and trade unions became more influential and the property-owning classes became increasingly nervous of what they saw as a revolutionary threat. The second consequence of industrial progress was the transformation of relations between nations. Germany, which been economically stagnant for much of the nineteenth century, was a great beneficiary of the second industrial revolution. This success was particularly marked in comparison with France. Between 1870 and 1914, French gross domestic product grew by an average of 1.6% per annum; German production grew by 2.8% per annum in the same period. This had important military implications. Germany had defeated France in 1870 and the two countries were to go to war again in 1914. Any shift in the relative economic strength of European nations risked upsetting the military order and provoking war. Just as French leaders looked nervously eastward at German economic growth, so German leaders looked nervously at the faltering beginnings of Russian industrialisation on their eastern frontier.

The spread of railways also changed military balances of power. Rail was becoming the main means of troop mobilisation. A.J.P. Taylor remarked that 1914 saw 'war by railway timetable.' Not everyone recognised the full importance of this development. Many were convinced that sea power was the key to great power status. Indeed this view was expressed in Arthur Mahan's work *The Influence of Sea Power upon History* (published in 1890). Mahan's interpretation was so influential that Kaiser Wilhelm II ordered a copy of his book to be placed on every German battleship. More importantly, Wilhelm and Admiral Tirpitz began to construct the large fleet which they believed Germany needed if she was to rival Great Britain. However, in reality, men began to believe in sea power at the very moment when it was ceasing to be important. The German fleet, which absorbed so many resources and created so much ill-will before the First World War, hardly left port between 1914 and 1918. Railways were far more important and they shifted power away from sea-bound nations, like Britain, towards continental powers at the centre of great land masses. Railways made central Asia more accessible, and the railways made it possible that the huge population of Russia could be brought west to fight a European war. Military, rather than economic, considerations encouraged French investors to fund the construction of the Russian railway network.

The spread of railways brought other changes in the lives of Europe. They created a new degree of national consciousness and integration. Daily newspapers became widely available, politicians were able to visit their constituencies. Even unified time zones were a creation of railways. Before their arrival, clocks in Limoges had been several minutes behind those of Paris. Railways also changed rural economies. The population around the Paris–Lyon–Marseilles railway line increased by about 25% as people moved to enjoy access to its benefits. Other forms of technology had a similar impact: the bicycle made even the most remote parts of rural France accessible to the, often competing, influences of parish priest and republican politicians. The Radical leader, Henri Queuille, used a bicycle to visit his constituents in Corrèze; the Catholic newspaper *La Croix* was sold by cycling vendors in rural Haute Savoie. It was entirely appropriate that the Tour de France became a symbol of the Republican integration of France.

If technology changed the way in which people lived, it had an even more dramatic impact on the way in which they could be killed. Breech loading rifles began to be used in 1860s, magazine (i.e. repeating) rifles came in the 1880s, as did smokeless powder (which made it possible for a rifleman to fire fast without blinding himself), and a variety of ever more sophisticated models of machine gun appeared in the run up to 1914. Weapons of this kind facilitated the conquest of Africa, and changed the battlefields of Europe. A range of brutally frank maxims circulated to describe the havoc wrought by rapid fire: 'We have the Maxim gun and they have not' (Belloc); 'le feu tue' (Pétain). However, the spread of military technology was often resisted by soldiers themselves. A survey conducted after the Franco-Prussian war showed that almost no one had been killed by bayonet. Yet as late as the Second World War, all infantry troops were given extensive training with a weapon that was, as George Orwell complained, 'useless for any purpose other than opening tins of corned beef'. Officers associated primitive weapons with the moral qualities of manliness and courage that were required of good soldiers.

Disputes about technology also became associated with the defence of the privileges of certain groups within the officer corps. In Prussia and Great Britain, the prestigious cavalry regiments were composed of poorly educated aristocrats who feared that technological modernisation might mean that they would be displaced by better educated, but socially inferior, officers from the artillery or engineers (70% of Prussian cavalry officers, but only 40% of artillery officers were from aristocratic backgrounds). The German navy made it clear that mere engineering officers were inferior to less specialized line officers (the former did not even get the right to wear officers' sashes until 1908). In France, by contrast, technical officers (often trained at the prestigious Ecole Polytechnique) were highly regarded: the artillery and engineering corps were more highly paid than other officers until late in the nineteenth century. Here opposition to technology came, not from aristocrats, but from the aged and uneducated captains and majors who had risen up from the ranks through hard work or battlefield experience. The Dreyfus case in France, when a Jewish officer was unjustly accused of leaking secrets to Germany in 1894, was a good example of the way in which technology could create conflicts within the officer corps. Dreyfus was a wealthy graduate of the Ecole Polytechnique who had become an artillery expert. General André, who subsequently purged the officer corps of anti-Dreyfusards, was also an artillery technocrat. By contrast, Major Henry, who denounced Dreyfus, was an infantry officer who had risen from the ranks.

Changes in military technology, and the disputes that arose

around such changes, increased international tensions. Governments became increasingly suspicious of the intentions and capabilities of their rivals. This suspicion underlay the spy mania that gripped Europe at the turn of the century. Tension was also increased by the resistance to technology that existed in so many armies. All officers, including those who worked most closely with new weapons, were fascinated by the mythology of a chivalrous warfare that they believed to have existed in the past. This partly accounted for the continued propensity of army officers to fight duels. When war broke out in 1914, many believed that it would give them a chance to display these chivalrous virtues. Students at the French officer academy at St Cyr vowed to go into battle in full dress uniform. It took four years of war to show how much machine guns, barbed wire and high explosives had changed the battlefield.

PART I
Towards Class War?

The issues between the conflicting forces of society are becoming narrower and more distinct. The mists of political theory are clearing away, and the true character of the battle-ground, and the real nature of the prize that is at stake, are standing out more and more distinctly every year. It galls the classes who barely sustain themselves by their labour that others should sit by and enjoy more than they do, and yet work little or not at all. Benighted enthusiasts in other lands, or other times, have struggled for idle theories of liberty or impalpable phantoms of nationality, but the 'enlightened selfishness' of the modern artisan now fully understands that political power, like everything else, is to be taken to the dearest market. He cares little enough for democracy unless it will adjust the inequalities of wealth. The struggle is now, in reality, when reduced to its simplest elements and stated in its most prosaic form, a struggle between those who have, to keep what they have got, and those who have not, to get it.

These words were written in 1860, by Lord Cranbourne, who later became the 3rd Marquis of Salisbury and the Conservative prime minister of Britain. Salisbury was a brilliant man, the only intellectual to have led the Conservative Party, and, like most intellectuals, he was wrong about everything. The period which opened in the 1860s did not see social issues displace all others and it finished not with a war between the classes but a war between the nations in which the workers, who were so feared by Salisbury, fought and died in loyal obedience to their social superiors. Salisbury's assumption that class conflict would be the dominant theme of politics in the late nineteenth century was shared by many Marxists. They assumed that society would become polarised between an industrial working class, or proletariat, which would possess nothing but their labour and a tiny group of magnificently rich capitalists who would preside over enormous factories. The former group having 'nothing to lose but their chains', would eventually rise up and destroy capitalism.

Marxist expectations about social conflict were wrong for several reasons. First of all, divisions that cut across class – such as religion, race and nationality – continued to be important. The persistence of the religious issue was most striking in France where the separation of Church and State in 1905 produced bitter conflict, and where bourgeois members of the Radical Party and working-class Communists were sometimes still united by anti-clericalism as late as the 1950s. Religion also mattered in Germany where Bismarck's *Kulturkampf* (1871–1891) alienated Catholics, and some Protestants who resented state interference into education. Many progressives were mystified by the continuing importance of religion, especially Roman Catholicism, in political life. They associated Catholicism with irrationality, superstition, traditionalism and everything that seemed alien to the modern world. In some ways the progress of nineteenth-century religious practice confirmed their view. Catholicism's appeal seemed to become less intellectual and more emotional as the century wore on. Pius IX's condemnation of liberalism, and his syllabus of errors published in 1864, created problems for liberal-minded intellectual Catholics such as the historian Acton. At the same time, the Church seemed increasingly dominated by the 'superstitions' of lower-class women and children. This tendency was exemplified by the increasing prominence that visions of the Virgin Mary began to assume in Catholic culture. Bernadette of Lourdes claimed to have seen such a vision in 1858, and by 1872, more than 110,000 people made pilgrimages to the shrine that was established there. In 1876 five girls claimed to have seen a similar vision in the village of Marpingen in the Saarland.

In some ways, of course, Catholicism survived precisely because it was able to appeal to groups – the poor, uneducated and female – who felt excluded from other institutions. Catholicism also turned out to be suited to the 'modern' world rather better than its self-consciously progressive enemies. Catholics believed in collective life not in liberal individualism: the Church was good at organising. Catholicism often became associated with the defence of groups, such as the peasantry or the artisans, that seemed threatened by economic modernisation. The Church acquired power in cities. When confused immigrants from Poland, or Ireland, or the Italian South, arrived in the industrial areas of Europe, and America, to seek work, they turned to the Church for solace and advice. Christian Democrat parties – such as the German Centre Party and the Austrian Christian Social Party – were founded. Such parties benefited from their cross-class appeal, and their hinge position in the political system (which allowed them to extract great concessions from government). They also displayed a striking talent for the distribution of state largesse to their clients and Tammany Hall political corruption. Christian Democracy was to increase in importance throughout the twentieth century and to become, after 1945, the dominant political force in Western Europe.

There were also purely social reasons why expectations about the onset of class war were proved wrong. Marxist assumptions about the nature of industrial concentration and class formation only really worked in the case of a few cities – Manchester in the early nineteenth century (the case study that had most influenced Marx); Roubaix in the late nineteenth century (where the *Marxist Parti Ouvrier Français* had its stronghold) and St Petersburg in the early twentieth century. In other cities, such as Birmingham or Lyon, small-scale industry remained important. Often large areas – such as the Italian South or the French South West – remained almost untouched by large-scale industry and such areas often exercised a political influence, especially in the age of universal suffrage, that counteracted the influence of both employers and workers in industry.

Most importantly, class conflict failed to materialize because of the survival of large numbers of small property owners. Some of these groups – such as the peasantry – had always existed. These groups managed to survive into the twentieth century partly because they displayed an unexpected ability to adjust to economic modernisation and partly because they managed to secure an important degree of political protection. However, a new lower middle class or petite bourgeoisie also emerged during the late nineteenth century. The lower middle class was created by several things. On the one hand the gradual separation of retail from production began to create the modern shopkeeper, while the concentration of retail in large stores (such as the Paris *Bon Marché* shops) created the modern shop assistant. On the other hand new industries and, most importantly financial companies, created a new need for large scale clerical employment.

There were considerable variations in the lives of members of the lower middle class. Independent shopkeepers often resented the security of clerks – especially clerical employees of the state whose leisurely life was financed by taxation. Bakers, who continued to be producers as well as retailers and who owned expensive equipment, were much wealthier than grocers. Even within clerical occupations, vast differences persisted: Leonard Bast, the clerk in E.M. Forster's *Howard's End*, lives with his mistress in a damp basement; Mr Pooter, hero of the Peabodys' *Diary of a Nobody*, lives in a semi-detached house with a wife and servant.

In spite of these variations, certain common features did unite the members of this class. They all worked in close proximity to their social betters, and they often shared certain external appearances with those betters – clean hands, respectable clothes, 'correct accents' – but, in terms of income, they often resembled the working class. This created a certain tension in the lives of many of the lower middle class. Members of this class were often infected by the romantic culture that spread through the educated classes during the nineteenth century: Bast listens to Beethoven and reads Ruskin. They were also fiercely ambitious; Mr Lewisham, the prep school teacher in H.G. Wells' *Love and Mr Lewisham*, rises at five in the morning to teach himself Latin. However, the reality of lower middle class life was strikingly unromantic and chances of social promotion were limited as the nineteenth century ended. Once clerking had been the first step in a process of social mobility. Clerks were trainees for higher positions – a practice that survives in the articled clerks of contemporary British solicitors and accountants. The expansion of clerical employment, and the increasing education of the upper middle class – meant that such opportunities were less likely to arise in future. Sometimes the petite bourgeoisie became fearful of the working class who seemed a social threat to their hard won respectability and a political threat to their interests. Such fears, and the propensity of the lower middle class to identify with their social superiors, made shopkeepers and clerical employees the natural constituency for popular conservatism that arose in many parts of Europe during the late nineteenth and early twentieth century. Such popular conservatism helped the ruling classes to avoid the conflicts of classes that Salisbury had foreseen in 1860, but it also carried new risks for the ruling classes. Popular conservatism was never wholly under the control of those who sometimes incited and benefited from it – this was a lesson that was to be learned by many industrialists and aristocrats from their dealings with fascism.

Robert Bideleux
Alexander II and the Emancipation of the Serfs

Robert Bideleux takes issue with some of the traditional views of the emancipation of Russia's serfs in 1861, and paints a more positive view of the emancipation and its effects than has often been the case.

Alexander II (reigned 1855–81) came to be known as the 'Tsar-Liberator' on account of his resoluteness in freeing millions of Russian serfs (bondsmen) through the 1861 Emancipation Act, amid widespread opposition from Russia's serf-owning nobility.

In 1850 peasants made up nearly 90% of Russia's population. Nearly half the peasantry, or about 38% of the total population, were serfs attached to private landed estates.[1] These serfs were required to provide their 'masters' with unpaid labour services (*barshchina*) and/or with dues in kind and/or cash quit-rents (*obrok*). They often provided a mixture of all three. Their lives were in large measure subject to their masters' wishes in such matters as choice of marriage-partner, occupation and place of residence. Serfs could be flogged or exiled to Siberia or sent into lengthy military service if they disobeyed their masters or endeavoured to run away, although it was usually in the masters' interests to use their powers sparingly. A serf-owner's wealth was usually reckoned in terms of the number of serfs under his jurisdiction. Most serfs were allocated farmland for their own use, on which to maintain themselves and raise (often large) families. Thus serfs, taken as a whole, became major producers in their own right. But a serf could always be transferred to landless domestic service or recalled to his master's estate whenever his master wished and any serf who became a successful trader or industrialist, as sometimes happened, usually had to pay dearly to obtain his personal freedom. But serfdom was not purely an economic institution. It was also an instrument of social control over a large and widely-scattered peasant population and a foundation stone of the Tsarist political system. This was why Alexander II's father and grandfather, Tsar Nicholas I (reigned 1825–55) and Tsar Alexander I (reigned 1801–25) respectively, had lacked the courage to dismantle serfdom, even though they came to see it as a social evil.

Reform before Emancipation

The other half of the peasantry largely consisted of 'state peasants' and, to a much lesser extent, 'crown peasants'. These were peasants resident on and attached to state land and the landed estates of the royal family, respectively. In Russia the state domain was far more extensive than privately-owned land. Although 'state peasants' and 'crown peasants' shared many of the obligations and disabilities of serfs, their position was on the whole more favourable. They usually received more land to cultivate for their own use, they were less likely to be required to provide labour services and their lives were less subject to external interference. Moreover, from 1837 onwards, 'state peasants' were placed under the jurisdiction of a new reform-minded Ministry of State Domains and Agriculture, established and administered by Count P.D. Kiselev. Kiselev endeavoured to distribute tax and quit-rent burdens more fairly, to make 'state peasants' less vulnerable to extortionate officials and middlemen and to prevent the emergence of a landless rural proletariat, by strengthening peasant communal institutions and communal landholding on the state domains, by moderating the revenue demands laid upon the 'state peasantry' and by fostering an enlightened (albeit paternalistic) code of conduct among his officials. Whereas the Ministry of Finance had previously tried to squeeze as much revenue as possible out of the 'state peasantry' in the short run, to the detriment of peasant welfare, agricultural productivity and incentives, Kiselev's new Ministry of State Domains and Agriculture aimed to develop peasant agriculture, protect peasant welfare and increase taxable incomes over a longer time-span. Indeed, the emancipation of the serfs in the 1860s should be seen as the natural sequel to Kiselev's reform of the state domains in 1837–55. (Nikolai Miliutin, one of the principal architects of the 1861 Emancipation Act, was a nephew and close disciple of Kiselev.)

The terms of Emancipation

Alexander II both freed Russia's serfs from personal servitude and endeavoured to ensure that they were 'allotted' sufficient land to meet their subsistence needs and their future financial obligations to the state, including so-called 'redemption payments' on the land allotted to them under the terms of the Emancipation. Overall, in 43 provinces of European Russia, the former serfs received 96% of the land they had previously farmed for their own use,[2] although there were significant regional variations. In eight Western provinces, whose predominantly Polish nobility staged a Polish nationalist rebellion against Tsarist rule in 1863, the terms of the

Emancipation were revised so as to punish the landed nobility by 'allotting' the former serfs more land than they had formerly cultivated for their own use, and in these Western borderlands the former serfs received their 'allotments' on more generous terms than elsewhere.

But in the fertile black earth and steppe provinces the former serfs were 'allotted' only 77% of the acreage they had previously cultivated for their own use, although terms of the transfer were more favourable than in the more northerly provinces. In the infertile and extensively forested Great Russian heartland, the former serfs received 'allotments' which were more generous in size but overpriced. Moreover, under agrarian legislation enacted in the mid-1860s, 'crown peasants' and 'state peasants' generally received 'allotments' which were both relatively large and more moderately priced. This was because the royal family and the state were less intent on exacting 'compensation' for the (less significant) loss of 'feudal' dues and labour-services than were the often heavily-indebted and spendthrift landed nobility. Also the crown lands and the state domains were mainly in Russia's more outlying or forested or infertile regions.

However, while such complex land transfers were bound to involve numerous anomalies, injustices and disputes, the fact that land was transferred to former serfs, 'state peasants' and 'crown peasants' on such a massive scale by such a notoriously oppressive and autocratic state was in itself remarkable and rather unusual. In many regions of Europe and the Americas, former serfs and slaves were freed either without land on which to support themselves or with severely inadequate landholdings, so as to create large pools of cheap and vulnerable wage-labourers and dependent share-croppers, who could easily be unscrupulously exploited by nearby landlords and employers. In Russia, even more remarkably, the ownership of the newly-established peasant 'allotments' was conferred, not on individual heads of household as private property but mainly on village communes as communal village property or, in regions where communal traditions were weak, or absent, on whole households as joint family property. In post-Emancipation Russia, peasant 'allotments' were farmed individually using family labour to meet family subsistence and financial needs, but they were not private property in the Western sense. 'Allotments' could not be bought, sold, mortgaged or distrained and, in most areas, they could be periodically reallocated or 'repartitioned' by the village assembly in response to changing local economic and demographic circumstances and in accordance with the peasants' own conceptions of equality and justice.

The Tsar-Liberator

At first sight, Alexander II was a most unlikely reformer. His stern and rigidly conservative father, Tsar Nicholas I, and his tutors had endeavoured to instil in him a devotion to the Imperial Army, to military pageantry and parades, and to the military virtues of obedience, order and discipline. Moreover, Alexander II always preferred riding and hunting to committees and affairs of state. He found it difficult to concentrate on serious business for long and his concentration was not helped by the gradual breakdown of his marriage to the Empress Marie and by persistent terrorist attempts to assassinate him during the 1860s and 1870s.

An important clue to his personality, which helps to explain why this otherwise conventional and conservative monarch instigated a fundamental 'restructuring' of Russian society, lay in his apparent thirst for approval and acclaim. This could be seen as weak-willed and as a source of psychological vulnerability, yet it motivated him to achieve things he would not otherwise have achieved. In his boyhood and youth, it was noted, he had always needed his austere and imposing father's approbation and praise. After his father's death, he sought the approval and acclaim of the relatives and friends whose qualities and judgement he most respected and who, it so happened, were mostly 'abolitionists'. Russian monarchs have usually paid little heed to what other people have thought of them, but Alexander II was an important exception.

The historiographic debate

Soviet and Western historians have argued endlessly over the motives, causes and wider significance of the emancipation of Russia's serfs. Taking their cues from Marx and Lenin, official Soviet histories of Russia have treated history as a teleological or sequential progression through successive forms of society or stages of development, each having its own distinctive prevailing 'mode of production' and 'dominant class'. The prime movers in this process are the 'class struggle' and the 'growth of society's productive forces'. Periods of transition from one state or form of society to the next are characterised by all-pervasive 'crises' of obsolescent 'modes of production' and 'accelerated evolution', and by the emergence of a new dominant class, a new prevailing 'mode of production' and new 'social relations' corresponding to the requirements of the next stage in the progression.

According to an official *History of the USSR* (Moscow, 1960), after 1800:

serfdom hampered the development of the productive forces of the country . . . hindered the growth of the home market, including the labour market, restricted the accumulation of capital and hampered the development of more progressive, capitalistic methods of production. The abolition of serfdom had become an absolute necessity. (p. 119)

The Emancipation was officially seen as the resolution of a deep-seated 'crisis of serfdom', marking the transition from 'feudalism' to 'capitalism'. But the embryo of capitalism was already growing within the womb of 'feudalism'. The 1830s mark 'the beginning of an industrial revolution', characterised by mechanisation and a transition from serf to wage labour in Russia's small but rapidly developing manufacturing sector; the rapid growth of towns and village industries; the emergence of a new class of capitalist forms of organisation (the factory and the joint stock company); a revolution in transport and communications (stage coach, steamboat, railway, postal and telegraphic services); and a transition from a relatively uncommercialised 'natural economy' to a commercialised market economy.

Soviet historians have claimed, not that mid nineteenth-century Russia was becoming an industrial country, but that revolutionary changes were taking place within the industrial and transport sectors, marking the beginning of capitalist industrialisation and a transformation of 'social relations'. The standard Western objections, that this industrialisation involved a narrow range of small-scale light industries with low levels of mechanisation, that Russia still lacked modern banks and significant steel, engineering, chemicals, coal and oil industries, and that Russia was still far from becoming an industrialised country, have rather missed the point. Until the 1820s the British Industrial Revolution was also based largely on sweated labour in a similarly narrow range of industries which also predated the railways and mainly consisted of small and relatively unmechanised workshops rather than factories, often located in rural areas with access to water power or wood fuel, yet this is still justifiably called the Industrial Revolution.[3]

Impact of industrialisation

Soviet historians of Russia have usefully demonstrated that pre-emancipation Russia was not quite as far behind the West as most Westerners like to think. Railways, steamboats, factories, steam-powered machinery and postal and telegraphic services appeared in Russia not more than two or three decades after their advent in the West. And Soviet historians have used one of several possible conceptions of an industrial revolution to characterise revolutionary changes which really did occur in Russia's small but rapidly developing industrial and transport sectors and which really did pose a significant threat or challenge to the continued existence of serfdom in Russia, in much the same way that the industrialisation of the northern United States threatened or challenged the continued existence of slavery in the 'Old South' during this same period. Indeed, the abolition of slavery in the USA and abolition of serfdom in Russia occurred almost simultaneously and, to a significant extent, Russian and American 'abolitionists' exchanged ideas and made common cause against the hated institutions of forced labour and personal servitude.

Up to a point, admittedly, capitalist industry based on wage labour could and did co-exist with systems of forced labour and personal servitude. But they represented rival economic systems and mutually incompatible moral values and conceptions of human rights, which is why 'abolitionism' was ultimately a moral issue and a moral crusade in both Russia and the USA.

The role of peasant unrest

According to official Soviet historiography the deepening 'contradictions' or tensions between the social order and 'social relations' based on serfdom and the 'developing productive forces' of capitalism produced 'an acute social and economic crisis'. This 'crisis of serfdom' gave rise to mounting peasant unrest, a 'revolutionary situation' and Russia's first major radical publicists and revolutionary thinkers – men such as Alexander Herzen (1812–70), Mikhail Bakunin (1814–76), Nikolai Chernyshevsky (1828–89) and Dmitri Pisarev (1840–68), who became the leading lights of the emerging radical intelligentsia. Moreover, following Russia's humiliating defeat in the Crimean War (1853–56), which cruelly exposed many of Russia's deficiencies and destabilised the economy and public finances, the Tsarist autocracy was 'forced to prepare the peasant reform of 1861'.

The Soviet emphasis on the importance of mounting peasant unrest and an emerging 'revolutionary situation' is, however, open to serious objections. The rising trend in peasant unrest is well-documented, but it fell far short of the more massive peasant unrest of the 1770s and the 1900s and does not constitute very convincing evidence of the existence of a 'revolutionary situation'. Moreover, while a radical intelligentsia and important revolutionary thinkers undoubtedly emerged amid the 'crisis of serfdom', no one has demonstrated that this was accompanied by the emergence of an organised revolutionary opposition capable of seizing power.

Furthermore, 'nothing in Alexander's private correspondence or in the reminiscences of his contemporaries supports the contention that the emancipation was the act of a frightened man', according to a leading authority on Tsar Alexander II.[4]

Indeed, Nicholas I and his advisers had regarded rising peasant unrest as a reason for delaying any radical restructuring of Russian society, because of the usefulness of serfdom as a form of control over the peasantry. 'The crucial significance of growing peasant unrest lay, not in its effects on Alexander II and his leading reformers, but in Alexander's skilful use of it to intimidate the conservative serf-owning nobility into reluctantly accepting the abolition of serfdom, above all in his famous warning that 'It is better to begin to abolish serfdom from above than to wait until it begins to abolish itself from below.'

The Crimean War

There is broader agreement on the importance of the Crimean War as a catalyst of reform. War is 'the midwife of progress' (Marx) and 'the locomotive of history' (Trotsky). The Crimean War highlighted deficiencies in Russia's industrial and armaments capacity, transport capabilities, morale, military reserves and ability to mobilise for war, which could only be overcome by a radical overhaul of the entire economic and social order. Significantly, some of the leading champions and agents of reform were drawn from the Navy Ministry, which drew radical conclusions from the Crimean débâcle. Serfdom came to be seen as incompatible with Russia's continuance as a Great Power.

There is also broad agreement on the importance of growing pressure for reform coming from educated public opinion and the press. Liberals, radicals, Slavophils, the Ministry of Foreign Affairs and leading members of the royal family shared a growing conviction that serfdom was an evil and morally indefensible institution, a source of shame and embarrassment and a blot on Russia's image abroad, barring it from the ranks of 'civilised' nations.

Success or failure?

The terms on which Russia's serfs were emancipated have incurred severe criticism, especially from the West. Most Western historians of Russia have taken the view that, by strengthening and extending the Russian village commune system and communal ownership of inalienable peasant 'allotments', and by making the membership of each village commune collectively responsible for taxes and for 'redeeming' the land allotted to them, the 1860s Emancipation perpetuated wasteful cropping patterns which impeded agricultural advance, penalised individual enterprise, imposed crushing financial burdens (the so-called 'redemption payments'), discouraged family-limitation and 'locked' the rapidly multiplying peasant population into an increasingly impoverished village sector, promoting rural over-population, famine and the peasant unrest which exploded in the early twentieth century.[5] As I have sought to demonstrate elsewhere, this dismal doom-laden view does not stand up to closer statistical investigation and it is possible to uphold much more positive 'revisionist' views of the post-Emancipation peasantry and peasant agriculture.[6] Professor A. Nifontov has estimated that, in 50 provinces of European Russia, the net output of grain and potatoes rose by 2% per annum from the 1860s to the 1890s, well ahead of population growth (1.3% per annum) and rural population growth (1.2% per annum), and Professor Paul Gregory has calculated that Russia's net output of grain and potatoes rose by over 3% per annum from 1885–89 to 1909–13.[7] Grain yields per hectare on European Russia's peasant 'allotments' rose almost as fast as those on private land from the 1860s to the 1900s, rose considerably faster than those of the West and Japan over the same period, kept ahead of rural population growth and by 1911–13 were comparable to those attained in other countries with similarly short and or moisture-deficient growing seasons. It is also questionable whether there really was a Russian 'famine' in 1891–92, as the above normal mortality at that time can be more plausibly attributed to the concurrent cholera epidemic, transmitted via Russia's unsanitary waterways and water-supplies.

Moreover, the financial burdens on the emancipated peasantry have also been exaggerated. The 'redemption payments' on land allotted to the peasantry were often burdensome and unjustly high at first, and peasants rightly resented having to pay anything at all for land which they regarded as having always been rightfully theirs (it had been 'usurped' by the state, the Tsars, the Church and the nobility in centuries past). But the inflation fuelled by large budget deficits, excessive printing of paper money and the bonds issued to former serf-owners as compensation for the land they had ceded to their former serfs steadily reduced the burden of redemption payments in real terms, as did the remissions granted in the 1880s, so that by the 1890s redemption payments represented under 10% of state revenue and under 2% of the value of agricultural output. By then all taxation amounted to under 13% of Russia's national income, which was comparable with Europe in general and well below the tax-burdens on most developing countries today.

	1860s	1870s	1880s	1890s
Population of European Russia (millions)	63.7	69.8	81.7	94.2
Net grain + potato output (million chetverts, grain equivalent)	158.0	187.0	228.0	290.5
– per inhabitant (chetverts)	2.5	2.7	2.8	3.1
– per rural inhabitant (chetverts)	2.8	3.0	3.2	3.6

Table 1: Net grain and potato output, European Russia, 1860–90.

	Russia	Europe (excl. Russia)	Southern Europe	Italy	Portugal	Greece	Spain	Japan	Austria-Hungary
1892–95	534	415	260	221	174	209	350	225	507
1909–13	555	411	276	274	160(a)	130(b)	400	240	508

	Bulgaria	Serbia	Romania	Denmark	France	Germany	Ireland	USA	Canada	Argentina
1892–95	–	–	780	1006	555	479	526	1291	1043	–
1909–13	545	470	880	852	514	595	633	1160(c)	1693(c)	1540

Table 2: Annual grain and potato output per inhabitant, Russia and other countries, 1892–1913.

Figures here represent kilograms, grain equivalent. As potatoes are 78% water and contain only one-quarter as many calories per kilogram as grain, four kilograms of potatoes have been treated as equivalent to one kilogram of grain. (a) 1918–22; (b) 1925–29; (c) 1911–13.

Demographic effects

It is also questionable whether the terms of the Emancipation really were responsible for rapid rural population growth. Private property prevailed in Finland and Romania, yet they experienced rates of rural population growth similar to Russia and countries such as Spain and Italy only avoided them thanks to mass emigration amongst their most fertile age-groups. There was nothing like the population explosion occurring in today's Third World. Moreover, Russia's Emancipation arrangements did not prevent dramatic increases in peasant mobility, reflected in the steep rise in the number of 'internal passports' issued to peasants each year (1.3 million in the 1860s, 7 million in the 1890s and 9 million in the 1900s). Mobility increased sufficiently to allow large-scale colonisation of Siberia, the Volga basin and the southern steppes and a

2.5% per annum growth of Russia's industrial proletariat between 1861 and 1914. Since industrial output grew by an impressive 5% per annum between 1861 and 1914, it is highly unlikely that Russia's towns and industries could have productively absorbed rural labour much faster than they did.

What the Emancipation arrangements did prevent was not the workforce-growth needed by Russia's burgeoning industries and expanding frontiers of agricultural settlement but a painful proletarianisation of the peasantry and a massive growth of vagrancy, slums, shanty towns and underemployed labour, such as occurred around many European cities in the nineteenth century and around many Third World cities in the twentieth century. Wage labourers made up under 10% of Russia's agricultural workforce as late as the 1900s and under 5% of peasant 'allotments' were smaller than 2.2 hectares (5.3 acres) according to the 1877 and 1905 land censuses. (By contrast, in France, Germany and Southern and Eastern Europe between one-third and two-thirds of all farms were smaller than 2.0 hectares and in Japan two-thirds were smaller than 1.0 hectares.)

Thus, notwithstanding frequent allegations that post-Emancipation Russia neglected the needs of the peasantry or lacked an effective agrarian policy, it can be seen to have had unusually enlightened agrarian arrangements which to a large extent shielded the peasantry against the usual dire social consequences of the rapid development of capitalism in an agrarian society, without significantly impairing the development of peasant agriculture and of the economy as a whole.

Indeed, by freeing peasants from the obligations to perform onerous unpaid labour-services and/or provide 'tribute' to serf-owners and/or the state, by transferring land to the tiller, and by allowing peasants to work their 'allotments' according to their own rights and using and reaping the rewards of their own family labour, the Emancipation released long-suppressed energies and initiatives, fostering an impressive growth and diversification of independent peasant agriculture. By 1881, 85% of former serfs had become owners of their 'allotments'.

An increasingly assertive peasantry

The irruptions of peasant unrest in the 1900s were rarely the result of impoverishment allegedly caused by the terms of the Emancipation. They were more often the result of the growing economic strength, assertiveness, education, confidence and expectations of the emancipated peasantry (albeit from small beginnings), major non-economic grievances and declining noble control of the countryside.

The dissolution of serfdom encouraged many estate-owners to

sell or lease out most of their land, especially as many invariably lived beyond their means or found themselves unable to generate enough cash to pay money wages to former serfs or discovererd that, in the absence of serfdom, they were often incapable of making a success of estate-management, since the Russian nobility was more strongly orientated towards careers in the army or public administration than entrepreneurship, and so was ill-equipped for the transition to capitalism.

The partial withdrawal of the nobility from the countryside into urban occupations increasingly brought discontented peasants into direct confrontations with the state, which had to rely increasingly on officials and the army to control the countryside. Thus local agrarian disputes became increasingly politicised and explosive. Moreover, the post-Emancipation peasantry continued to be subject to widely-resented legal civil disabilities and, in addition, over half the peasantry belonged to underprivileged and oppressed ethnic and or religious minorities, who increasingly asserted their separate identities, aspirations and demands, from the 1890s to 1917.

Unfinished business

Thus, although the agrarian arrangements established by the Emancipation of the serfs were unusually enlightened, the 'Tsar-Liberator' left a lot of unfinished business, raised expectations which his regime was unable to fulfil and released social forces which it was ultimately incapable of controlling (foreshadowing Russia's more recent experience of 'perestroika' under Mikhail Gorbachev). Alexander II was assassinated at the seventh attempt by revolutionary terrorists who believed that his reforms had not gone far enough and that his death would trigger off a more far-reaching social revolution. Instead, the assassination of the 'Tsar-Liberator' precipitated a reactionary backlash against the intelligentsia and ethnic and religious minorities and a reversal of some of his reforms, deflecting Russia off the road towards freedom and on to the road towards a modern police state and new forms of serfdom. Alexander II's life ended not just in personal tragedy, but in a tragedy from whose consequences Russia is still struggling to escape.

Notes

(1) Hoch, H. and Augustine, W. 'The tax censuses and the decline of the serf population of Imperial Russia 1833–58', *Slavic Review*, Vol. 38 (1979), pp. 403–25.

(2) Gerschenkron, A. 'Agrarian policies and industrialisation in Russia 1861–1917', in *Cambridge Economic History of Europe*, Vol. 6, Part II (Cambridge University Press, 1966).

(3) Berg, M. *The Age of Manufacturers* (Fontana Press, 1985).
(4) Kieber, A. *The Politics of Autocracy* (Mouton and Co., 1966) p. 133.
(5) Gerschenkron, A. 'Agrarian policies and industrialisation in Russia 1861–1917', in *Cambridge Economic History of Europe*, Vol. 6, Part II (Cambridge University Press, 1966); Robbins, R.G. *Famine in Russia* (Columbia University Press, 1975).
(6) Bideleux, R. *Communism and Development*, (Methuen, 1987) pp. 11–22, 32–3, 45; Bideleux, R. 'Agricultural advance under the Village Commune System', in Bartlett, R. (ed.) *Land Commune and Peasant Community in Russia* (Macmillan, 1990) pp. 196–218.
(7) Nifontov, A.S. *Zernovoe proizvodstvo Rossii vo vtoroi polovine XIX veka*, (1974), pp. 198–201, 284–7; Gregory, P. 'Grain marketings and peasant consumption in Russia 1885–1913', in *Explorations in Economic History*, Vol. 17 (1980) pp. 135–64.

Robert Bideleux is the Director of the Centre of Russian and East European Studies at the University College of Swansea, University of Wales. His principal publication is *Communism and Development* (Methuen, 1987).

Lee Emerson
Tolstoy and Tsarism

What can we learn from the picture of Tsarist Russia on the verge of the 1905 Revolution as depicted in Tolstoy's novel Resurrection, *and how reliable is the picture that emerges?*

Tolstoy's novel *Resurrection* (first published in 1899)[1] offers a graphic portrayal of Tsarist Russia as it lurched towards revolutionary chaos in 1905. Indeed, Russian literature from the nineteenth century occupies a unique position in helping us to understand what was happening to that ill-fated country. Unlike most other countries in Europe, Russia possessed no national representative assembly where the voice of dissent could be heard. Even in the German Empire created by Bismarck, there was some acknowledgement of the need to allow a degree of criticism to be voiced, albeit from a fairly impotent Reichstag. But in Russia, the refusal of the Tsars to permit even this basic concession stifled open political debate, and led to the formation of a clandestine revolutionary movement wholly committed to the destruction of its persecutors, usually by violence. It was in this vacuum of political debate that Tolstoy and others wrote their novels, dealing with issues of contemporary importance to their readership. Not surprisingly, these books took on a political aspect, offering many Russians a chance to read criticisms of their government and society that were not otherwise available to them. Despite the backwardness of Tsarist society, many ordinary Russians showed a considerable appetite for books, suggesting the written word was far more powerful a weapon than is often assumed. Westwood's figures show that whereas in 1855, 1,020 book titles were published in Russia, by 1894 this figure stood at 10,691, equal to the total output in the USA and Britain combined;[2] thus, while appreciating the window into Russia's soul that Tolstoy offers, it is important to recognise that his writing was in his own time also a potent political weapon.

The Orthodox Church and the legal system

In his later years, Tolstoy had become an inveterate enemy of the Tsarist regime. His chief novel in these years was *Resurrection*, set in the 1880s. Parts of this book were so politically explosive that they were immediately cut from the original edition by the censor. Nevertheless, a full Russian edition was published in London the

to complete destruction . . . Cast away from [Thy people] the intolerable oppression of officials. Destroy the wall between Thyself and Thy people and let them rule the country together with Thyself.[3]

The events of 1905 that followed in Russia show clearly Tolstoy's ready appreciation of the deep frustration felt towards this dehumanised body of people – this 'wall' of Russian officialdom.

Political prisoners in Tsarist Russia

From this point, Tolstoy proceeds through his hero Nekhlyudov, to consider more closely the motives behind those prisoners in the convoy who are termed 'politicals'. Regarding them at first with dislike and contempt, he comes to sympathise with their cause as he gets to know them, and the senseless way in which the government has driven them to such extreme lengths:

> These people were like fish taken in a net: the whole catch is landed, the big fish are sorted out and the little ones are left to perish on the shore. Similarly, hundreds of people, who were obviously not merely innocent but who could in no way be dangerous to the government, were arrested and held in prison, often for years . . . The fate of these people – often innocent even from the government point of view – depended on the whim, leisure or humour of some police officer or spy or public prosecutor, or magistrate or governor or minister . . . The political offenders were treated like enemies in wartime, and they naturally used the same methods that were used against them.

Tolstoy's own conclusion appears to be that the revolutionaries deserve better understanding from those who would condemn their actions out of hand. Tolstoy himself never advocated violence; but the repulsion he felt towards the arbitrary and totally unjustified behaviour of the state leaves us in no doubt on which side his sympathies lay. He cites some individual examples which move the reader to some sympathy. There was the student, Kryltsov, who was successful in his academic studies and had fallen in love with a girl he was considering marrying. He was asked by some fellow students for a contribution to 'the cause', and for no particular good reason he gave them some money, even though he took no interest in their activities. Those collecting were caught, a note was found showing that money had been given by Krylstov, and the poor student found himself deported to hard labour in Siberia and suffering from consumption as a result of his treatment. In another incident, two Polish youths had been arrested with Polish proclamations in their pockets, and then executed after having tried to escape from the convoy taking them to the railway station. Such examples, even allowing for the emotive way in which Tolstoy depicts them, provoke the conscience of the reader, and while the characters are fictional there is little doubt that the situations are not intended to be extraordinary. Such a state of affairs highlights for us the integral role of the Russian State in bringing about its own downfall, foreshadowed in 1905, just a few years after the publication of *Resurrection*.

The peasant question

In another of his digressions from the main plot, Tolstoy delves into the peasant problem. In his own life, this was a question that troubled him greatly, and he came to belong to that class of noble who was riddled with guilt over his participation in the system that oppressed the great majority of the Russian people. His views are faithfully reproduced by Nekhlyudov, whose soul searching leads him to the socialist ideas of Henry George and the conclusion that 'everyone has an equal right to land and to all the benefits that can be derived from it'. However, Tolstoy is not blinkered when he portrays the Russian peasant in his writing – he knew them too well to harbour any illusions. Tolstoy's peasants are grizzled, disgruntled and ungrateful, seemingly incapable of lifting their horizons above the banalities of life on the land. Perhaps one of the most depressing episodes in the book is the reaction of the peasants to Nekhlyudov's offer of distributing all his remaining land to them in return for a very small rent:

> As always, though it was much lower than other rents paid in the neighbourhood, the peasants began to haggle and to find the figure too high. Nekhlyudov had expected that his offer would be welcomed with delight, but no signs of pleasure were visible. Only one thing showed Neklyudov that his offer was to the peasants' advantage, and that was the bitter disputes which broke out when the question of who should rent the land was discussed: should it be the whole commune or a representative body from each village? The peasants in favour of keeping out the feeble and the poor payers argued fiercely with those they wanted to exclude . . .

Tolstoy also has something to contribute to the debate, aired in the earlier article by Robert Bideleux, on the welfare of the serfs after emancipation. Bideleux argues that the condition of the peasants after emancipation was not as bad as traditional western historiography has portrayed it, and he puts forward evidence to suggest a degree of prosperity in the years following 1861. Tolstoy's view was less optimistic. The land he refers to in the following excerpt is in the black soil belt (i.e. the richer type of soil found in Russia):

> He [Nekhlyudov] had lived on this estate in his childhood and youth, and had been there twice since. On one occasion, at his mother's request, he had taken a German bailiff with him and had gone over the whole property, so that he was familiar with the condition of the estate and knew the relations the peasants bore to the *office* [landlord]. These relations were such that the peasants were – to put it nicely – entirely dependent on his management, or – to speak plainly – in a state of servitude to the office. It was not active serfdom such as had been abolished in the year 1861 (the thraldom of certain persons to their master) but a general state of serfdom among persons owning no land, or very little, *vis-à-vis* the great landlords in general and primarily, and sometimes solely, those among whom the peasants lived. Nekhlyudov knew this, he could not be ignorant of it, since the economy of his estates was based on this serfdom, and he had assisted in the setting up of this economy.

Of course, this view is not based on research and statistical evidence, as is much of the current debate: but it is rooted in Tolstoy's personal experience of landowning, and taken in conjunction with other evidence, provides a significant argument against the revisionists. Moreover, bare statistics rarely tell the whole picture: peasant life after emancipation was often determined by factors that were peculiar to each estate and which are therefore impossible to quantify – in the above excerpt there is the example of the crafty German bailiff who (it transpires) has been fleecing the peasants for all they were worth in the absence of the landlord. Tolstoy cites further examples:

> Moreover, the peasants paid with their labour – and dearly too – for everything they got from the estate. They paid with their labour for the use of meadow-land, for wood and potato tops, and nearly all of them were in debt to the office. Thus the peasants paid four times as much for the land which they rented beyond the cultivated fields as the owner could have got by selling it and investing the proceeds at 5%.

This does not answer whether or not the peasants were producing more food or not, but it provides a compelling argument that their overall position had hardly improved since emancipation.

Conclusion

Using novels as historical evidence is often a problematic exercise, and some may think Tolstoy's word has here been taken too much at face value in his denigration of the society from which he did in any case feel such alienation. On the other hand, Tolstoy was a serious writer for whom truth was absolute and real, and whose work had to bear some relation to reality in order for it to be accepted by his countrymen. How, then, should we assess the usefulness of this novel?

In the first place, it should broaden our awareness of some of the processes taking place in Russia. What people felt and experienced, and which often filled them with indignation towards the regime, was often just as important as the great historical events which fill the pages of history. The everyday operations of government officials impinged far more on the lives of ordinary Russians than the actions of diplomats or the outcome of battles in faraway places. In particular, the novel could help explain the feelings and attitudes of many Russians towards their government as the turbulent period of revolution dawned in 1905.

Secondly, the book helps us understand something of the deep alienation towards the regime felt by the Russian intelligentsia. These radical intellectuals acted as a sort of conscience in the Russian soul, and Tolstoy's moral rejection of Tsarism and its trappings (along with that of others) was an important factor in the regime's loss of standing, both at home and abroad. Perhaps again the pen has proved mightier than the sword.

Notes

(1) All excerpts from *Resurrection* by Leo Tolstoy are from the Penguin edition, translated by Rosemary Edmonds and first published in 1966.
(2) Westwood, J.N. *Endurance and Endeavour* (Oxford University Press, 1981).
(3) Kertesz, G.A. (ed.) *Documents in the Political History of the European Continent 1815–1939* (Oxford University Press, 1968).

Lee Emerson is Head of History at Portsmouth Grammar School.

David Kirby
The Second International

The late nineteenth century saw a dramatic rise in the prominence of socialist parties across Europe. But in the face of the First World War, international socialism proved impotent and the movement itself was subsequently split by the rise of revolutionary communism.

Judged solely in terms of its growth during the first 25 years of its existence, the Second International was truly an impressive creation. On the eve of the First World War, this international organisation of socialist and workers' parties could boast an affiliated membership of over three million. Under its auspices, the various factions of the left in France had united in 1905 as the French Section of the Second International (SFIO), and in the 1914 elections to the Chamber of Deputies had won 103 seats. The German Social Democratic Party (SPD) had made even more striking advances, winning the support of one in three of those voting in the Reichstag elections of 1912. With over a million members, for whom it provided a wide range of activities and, indeed, a veritable 'alternative culture', the SPD was regarded as the jewel in the crown of the Second International. Its theorists and spokesmen were listened to with respect as the foremost exponents of Marxism; their pronouncements set the tone for other European social democratic parties. The words of Karl Kautsky, the foremost Marxist theoretician of his day, were avidly digested even by the quarrelsome Russian socialists, pursuing their internal feuds in impoverished exile in Paris or Zurich. With the exception of the British Isles, where Marxist ideas and social democracy failed to flourish, socialism appeared to be advancing inexorably towards final victory (or at least electoral success) almost everywhere in Europe and was making headway in Asia and the Americas. The member parties of the Second International, publicly committed to opposing war and the machinations of the Great Powers, could justifiably claim that they constituted a powerful force for peace; and yet, when the crisis finally erupted in the summer of 1914, the movement was revealed not only as impotent to act, but also to be badly divided along national, and even nationalistic lines.

Origins

The First International, or the International Working Men's Association, founded in 1864 by a curious coalition of British trade unionists and European socialists of various hues under the guidance of Karl Marx, had not been a success. At first, it seemed as if the Second International would also disintegrate into squabbling factions; but during the 1890s, social democratic and socialist parties began to acquire a significant following and, more importantly, a firm organisational structure and an ideology. In this respect, the lifting of the anti-socialist laws in Imperial Germany in 1890 following the downfall of Bismarck was of great significance, for it allowed the SPD once more to operate freely on German soil. Condemned by the passing of the anti-socialist laws in 1878 to twelve years of persecution and exile, the party had developed a greater sense of purpose and discipline. In Karl Kautsky, it had also acquired a leading exponent of Marxist ideas, and it was Kautsky who was largely responsible for the theoretical preamble to the SPD's 1891 Erfurt programme. This classic statement of Marxist principles was subsequently copied and adopted by many other European social democratic parties, and although challenged by so-called 'revisionists' such as Eduard Bernstein, and later by left-wingers such as Rosa Luxemburg, the interpretations of Marxist thought laid down by Kautsky prevailed as an accepted orthodoxy right up until the First World War. Kautsky was respected and admired even by Vladimir Ilyich Lenin, later to become his most bitter opponent.

The organisational structure of the Second International was given greater permanence in 1900, when the Paris congress established a secretariat and offices in Brussels and appointed an International Bureau composed of representatives of the major parties, with directions for regular meetings for the preparation and expedition of business. The appointment in 1905 of Camille Huysmans as secretary of the International further raised the profile of the movement, for the young Belgian socialist was an intensely active figure, amassing huge amounts of documentary material and bombarding member parties with questionnaires and directives. Huysmans was to play an important role in efforts to reconvene the International Bureau during the war, and his significance in the movement is only now being appreciated.

'Ever onward, ever upward'

It was, however, at the congresses of the International that the great issues of the day were publicly debated; and within the intense, serious world of the socialist movement, such matters as the length of the working day, military service, colonialism and, above all, the avoidance of war, were endlessly worked over. There was little room for frivolity or light relief in the columns of the socialist press, or on the agenda of meetings in countless workers' halls, committee rooms and the often very impressive regional headquarters of the socialist parties. Imbued with a spirit of moral righteousness, fired with the ideals of scientific advancement which could liberate mankind, and driven by a sense of social justice, these heavily-bearded, unsmiling gentlemen (and note the relative lack of women delegates) captured by the camera for posterity as they assemble for their meetings sincerely believed that the world was going their way – that the future lay with socialism. They were assured by the rising curve of support and the truly impressive growth of the labour movement, whose imagery and vocabulary were replete with 'progressive' terms. *Vorwärts, Avanti!, Forward*, were the titles of the main newspapers of the SPD, the Italian socialists and the Independent Labour Party in Britain, and the slogan 'ever onward, ever upward' reflected this sense of unstoppable advance to the goal of socialism. The vocabulary of the labour movement was also bellicose. The language of the class struggle and merciless conflict with the forces of capitalism at times contrasted oddly with the messages of fraternity, humanity and pacifism emanating from the councils of the socialists.

There was indeed a wide and growing gulf between the rhetoric, the self-generating mythology of the Second International, and the reality of the situation. In the first place, despite the advances made at the polls and in the factories and workshops, the vast majority of working-class men and women remained either indifferent or hostile to socialism. The difficulties faced by a committed socialist in trying to win over fellow-workers are graphically described in Robert Tressell's novel, *The Ragged-trousered Philanthropists*. In France on the eve of world war, trade union militants complained that the workers preferred to play cards or read smutty literature than join the union or attend meetings, and there were similar worries in other countries that the movement was beginning to lose support.

Committed to winning power by the ballot-box, often in countries where the electoral system was far from democratic and where parliamentary control of government did not exist, encountering unremitting hostility from the ruling classes, socialist leaders did occasionally doubt whether they would ever attain their objectives. The 'working classes' which they claimed to represent were disciplined, organised forces, not an uncontrollable mass, whose revolutionary 'spontaneity' (idealised by the left) was anathema to the moderate leadership. Some of the Scandinavian social democratic leaders openly championed alliance with reformist bourgeois parties in order to win parliamentary and suffrage reform, in spite of the fact that the entry into government of the French socialist Alexandre Millerand in 1899 had prompted a furious debate within the ranks of the International and had resulted in a resolution condemning socialist participation in government under capitalism. Some were even contemplating the possibility of moving away from an exclusive working-class base of support towards the notion of a 'people's party' which might appeal to disaffected lower middle-class votes. In spite of the impressive array of statistics showing growing electoral support, there was a good deal of unease about the future within the labour movement as it entered the second decade of the twentieth century.

War on war

This unease also surfaced in connection with the debate on war, which increasingly occupied the attention of the Second International. The founding congress in Paris (1889) had declared unequivocally that wars would only disappear with the triumph of socialism and the emancipation of labour from the shackles of capitalism. The International nevertheless over the next two decades embraced a series of measures designed to prevent war: people's militias to replace standing armies, disarmament, obligatory arbitration of international disputes, parliamentary controls over foreign policy, and the right to national self-determination. Similar sanctions and controls were also demanded by many radical liberals, and were taken up by President Wilson of the United States in the closing stages of the First World War. Such proposals were regarded by those on the left of the labour movement as mere palliatives. The general consensus within the international labour movement was that its massive combined forces ought to be mobilised to combat any threat of war. The notion of a general strike was advanced by Keir Hardie and the French socialist Eduard Vaillant at the 1910 Copenhagen congress of the International as a 'particularly efficacious' means of preventing or hindering war; but the meeting did not take up the idea. At the Stuttgart congress three years earlier, the left had managed to slip in an amendment to the main resolution, which declared that, should war break out, socialists should take measures to bring about its early termination 'and strive with all their power to use the economic and political crisis created by the war to arouse the masses politically and to hasten the overthrow of capitalist class rule'. This passed virtually unnoticed; as the historian Georges Haupt commented, it committed the delegates to nothing for the foreseeable future.

As the stormclouds gathered, the International continued to boom out its anti-war message – nowhere more dramatically than in Basel in November 1912, during the Balkan Wars. Assembled in emergency congress with remarkable speed and efficiency, delegates from 23 socialist parties presented a resolute and united front, dedicated to combating the imminent threat of war. The resolution adopted by the congress denounced that threat in ringing tones, and assigned tasks to the socialist parties of the individual countries: it called for an extension of anti-war propaganda, but it failed to come up with any clearcut guidelines as to what the organised proletariat should do to prevent war. In an article published just after the Basel congress, the Austrian socialist Otto Bauer drew attention to the fact that the power of the state was at its greatest, and national passions at their height, on the outbreak of war. To attempt to stage a general strike in such circumstances would be a 'utopian fantasy'. Even if the International Bureau could co-ordinate a general strike on an international scale, argued the French socialist leader Jules Guesde early in 1914, the inequality in strength of the labour movements in the various countries would imperil the existence of the most powerful, and socialism itself. Similar objections were raised by German socialists, uncomfortably aware of the weakness of the labour movement in Russia.

Nevertheless, as the crisis unfolded during the long, hot days of July 1914, the labour movement strove valiantly to uphold the cause of peace. Massive anti-war rallies were held, the socialist press warned of the dangers and horrors of war; the French socialist Jean Jaurès, one of the most passionate and persuasive advocates of the cause of peace, strove unceasingly to defuse the situation. At the end of the month, the crisis suddenly accelerated, catching the socialist movement (and others) by surprise. A meeting of the International Bureau was hastily convened in Brussels on 29–30 July. The mood of the delegates reflected the general confusion. The veteran, Victor Adler, opened the discussion with a blunt declaration that his Austrian social democratic party was powerless, unable to stem the tide of pro-war sentiment; Hugo Haase for the SPD chided the Austrians for their passivity and spirit of resignation, and spoke of massive anti-war demonstrations in Germany. The meeting ended with the adoption of a resolution calling upon the workers to intensify their efforts to prevent war; but no further measures other than an emergency congress to be held the following week in Paris were proposed.

On 31 July, Jean Jaurès was shot outside a Parisian cafe by a nationalist fanatic. The sudden removal from the scene of the man who epitomised the socialist anti-war movement added a touch of high drama to events, but did little to influence them. Jaurès was as committed to the defence of the revolutionary fatherland as anybody. After a hurried and inconclusive meeting with the German party secretary, Hermann Müller, on 1 August, the SFIO leadership invoked the name of their murdered leader in declaring their readiness to defend France. Moreover, they proclaimed this as 'keeping faith with the revolutionary tradition of socialism and the International'. Two days later, Germany declared war on France, and the SPD parliamentary group agreed, with only 14 dissentient voices, to vote for war credits in the Reichstag the following day. It fell to Hugo Haase, one of the 14 and the party vice-chairman, to justify the SPD's unanimous vote of support with the words: 'we are doing what we have always proclaimed: in the hour of danger, we will not leave the fatherland in the lurch.' Within a month, the labour movements of all the belligerent countries, with the exception of the small Serbian socialist party and most of the Russian socialist groupings, had aligned themselves with the war effort, concluding an informal political truce for the duration. Socialists accepted government office in Belgium and France in the autumn of 1914, and representatives of the Labour Party entered government in Britain after May 1915. Several who had vehemently opposed all forms of militarism and war suddenly became ardent patriots; others were dismayed and in some cases driven to contemplating suicide. Those who detected a new revolutionary epoch dawning, as did Lev Davidovich Trotsky in the autumn of 1914 (in his pamphlet, *The War and the International*), were few in number and almost entirely isolated from the mainstream of international social democracy.

The International and the War

Once the first shock had passed, there was a wave of indignation amongst those who still opposed the war, such as Russian socialists, for whom the proud banner of international socialism had been shamefully disgraced by the cowardly actions of those 'social patriots' who now supported the war efforts of their governments. It was amongst these circles, supported by left-wing socialists of the neutral countries, that attempts to revive the spirit of internationalism were first made in the winter of 1914–15, culminating in the holding of a conference at the Swiss village of Zimmerwald in September 1915. The revival of the anti-war movement, which was to bear the name of this village, was by no means the only sign of activity. Camille Huysmans valiantly attempted to maintain contact with the now divided affiliated member parties of the International, and risked the wrath of his Belgian colleagues by agreeing to the transfer of the headquarters of the International Bureau to neutral Holland. Before the end of 1916, little progress was made. Growing war weariness, rising domestic discontent and political unease eroded the hitherto dominant status of the most intransigent supporters of the war effort. The appeal of President Wilson to the belligerents to consider a peace without victors or vanquished was taken up by sections of the French and Italian labour movements in the early months of 1917. The triumph of the forces of democracy over autocracy in Russia and the ringing call of the Petrograd Soviet for a general peace brought about a dramatic revival of international socialist efforts, which focused on the city of Stockholm in neutral Sweden. Joining forces with the Scandinavian socialists, Huysmans and his Dutch colleagues issued an invitation to an international socialist conference; the Zimmerwald movement, which also transferred its activities to the Swedish capital, also called for a conference of those opposed to the war. At the same time, the Petrograd Soviet was busily engaged in discussions with Allied socialist leaders in an effort to persuade them to endorse the idea of a negotiated peace.

These activities reached their peak in the spring of 1917. Austria-Hungary was on the verge of collapse. Germany was racked by strikes after a winter of privation and hardship which had finally blown asunder all notions of common sacrifice for the war effort. Large sections of the French army on the Western front were in a state of mutiny. In such circumstances, the war leaders were disposed to play along with the clamour for negotiations, and used the moderate socialists as agents for this purpose. The great enthusiasm for peace was not however channelled into any movement powerful enough to compel governments to the peace table. The Stockholm conference did not take place (though the Zimmerwaldists did hold a meeting in September, and endorsed a proposal for a simultaneous international general strike against war). The French government recovered its nerve under the iron grip of a new premier, Georges Clemenceau, and the renewed appeal of the Bolshevik regime in Russia for a general peace was ignored by the Allies. The British labour movement, which had hitherto taken little interest in foreign affairs, now took up the question of a future peace settlement, and the memorandum adopted by the inter-allied socialist conference in February 1918 was predicated on the assumption that Imperial Germany first must be defeated before the world could be made safe for democracy. The preventive strategy endorsed by the Second International at its Copenhagen congress in 1910 was embedded in the allied socialists' memorandum; indeed, many of the democratic and progressive ideals of pre-war socialism were taken up in the immediate post-war years. The more militant 'curative' strategy of the Zimmerwald movement, which sought to end the threat of war by revolutionary mass action, also survived, even though the movement as such was formally pronounced defunct by the Communist (Third) International, founded in Moscow in March 1919.

Socialist internationalism and the legacy of 1914

August 1914 has always been regarded as the great watershed in the history of socialist internationalism, largely because the historical agenda has usually been set by those who regret or deplore the inability of the Second International to act decisively. Now that the direct legacy of 1917 has finally perished, it may be possible to re-evaluate the nature of the labour movement more dispassionately, and to overcome the barriers which the voting for war credits symbolically created for the left. Notwithstanding the wide spectrum of opinion and attitudes within the forces of the Second International, it was pre-eminently a movement for change, radical change, and was resolutely opposed to the existing order. Rallying to the defence of one's country in 1914 did not imply sudden abandonment of opposition to the existing order; indeed, for many, the struggle assumed new dimensions, and the changed situation held out new possibilities. The revolutionaries were not the only ones who sniffed change in the air; the right-wing German social democrat Eduard David detected a mood for democratic change at the very beginning of the war, for example, and the collectivist experience of mass mobilisation not only gave rise to an immense amount of theorising about the future role of the state, but also gave trade unionists and party officials a chance to savour the exercise of power and to note the opportunities this opened up.

It is tempting to say that the only ones who learnt nothing from the wartime experience were those who opposed the war, but were contemptuously dismissed by Lenin as 'social pacifists', 'wretched men in mufflers' who slept with 'the old, shabby book of official socialism under their pillow': but they were nonetheless the principal upholders of the ethical, oppositional socialist internationalism first expounded by Karl Marx in his Address to the founding congress of the First International. Marx urged the working class 'to watch the diplomatic acts of their respective governments; to counteract them, if necessary, by all means in their power, when unable to prevent, to combine in simultaneous denunciations, and to vindicate the simple laws of morals and justice, which ought to govern the relations of private individuals, as the rules paramount of the intercourse of nations.' The failure of the Second International to stop war in 1914 was a setback, certainly, but by no means a shattering blow. And, perhaps, posterity has some reason to be grateful to those serious-minded earnest advocates of peace for keeping alive the cause of sanity and humanity in a world plunged into destruction.

Further Reading

Braunthal, J. *History of the International*, Vol. I. 1864–1914 (Nelson, 1966).

Carsten, F.L. *War against War: British and German Radical Movements in the First World War* (Batsford, 1982).

Haupt, G. *Socialism and the Great War: The Collapse of the Second International* (Oxford University Press, 1972).

Joll, J. *The Second International 1889–1914* (Routledge and Kegan Paul, 1974).

Kirby, D.G. (1986) *War, Peace and Revolution: International Socialism at the Crossroads, 1914–18* (Gower, 1986).

David Kirby teaches History at the School of Slavonic and East European Studies, University of London.

John Maher
Anarchism

There is much more to anarchism than the terrorist stereotype of late nineteenth-century legend.

Studies of anarchism often begin by remarking on the popular image of the bomb-thrower. They stress the inaccuracy of this stereotype, and emphasise the philosophical antecedents of the movement, perhaps mentioning the Stoics and Hedonists of Ancient Greece, passing through some medieval Christian sects, before concentrating on the central influence of early socialist thinkers such as William Godwin and Pierre-Joseph Proudhon.[1] Only then is the reader introduced to Mikhail Bakunin, the founder of modern anarchism as a political movement rather than a philosophical ideal, and incidentally, largely responsible for that popular caricature of the anarchist conspirator.

This article will begin with Bakunin, stressing that it is with him, and his ability to attract a revolutionary following, that a distinct anarchist politics emerged. Bakunin was equally significant in establishing the other central feature of anarchist identity, the mutual antagonism between anarchists and orthodox Marxists.

Bakunin was a gigantic Russian of aristocratic descent, whose extravagant personality, love of conspiracy, secret societies and revolutionary drama made him Europe's best-known revolutionary after 1848. His personality and politics were very different to those of his contemporary, Karl Marx, and their conflict expresses some of the questions at the heart of revolutionary socialism.

The polemic between Bakunin and Marx was fought out most vividly between 1869 and 1872 in the International Working Men's Association (IWMA) known as the First International. This organisation was founded in 1864. In 1868, Bakunin – with his followers – attempted to join, to Marx's horror, since he regarded Bakunin and his beliefs as a liability to the socialist movement. When Bakunin gained admission in 1869, Marx and Engels became engaged with the Bakuninists in a struggle for leadership. By the time Bakunin was expelled in 1872, the First International had been torn apart in the archetypal socialist fratricide.[2]

Anarchism and Marxism

Marxism and anarchism had much in common. Both developed with the labour movement in the nineteenth century, and both argued for a social and political revolution in which the workers would overthrow the capitalist state. Anarchist criticism of Marx was based on the rejection of his materialist conception of history – the idea that societies advanced through a series of historical stages based on their economic modes of production, each stage emerging from its predecessor and culminating inexorably in communism.[3] This was criticised by anarchists as being too rigid and historically inaccurate, as well as subordinating revolutionary *élan* to what they dismissed as 'scientific socialism'.

It is from this fundamental disagreement that the anarchist critique of Marxist theory and practice derives. It led to the anarchists' rejection of Marx's theory of revolution, especially the advocacy of a period of dictatorship of the proletariat in a workers' state before the state's final 'withering away'. Bakunin and his followers aimed at the immediate and total destruction of the state along with capitalism, insisting that the new society could not be born out of the structures of the old. Marxists, meanwhile, criticised anarchists for seeing the state as the cause of injustice and exploitation, rather than as a political structure based on the economic system. Hence, Marxists could accept that a proletarian revolution would be accompanied by a strengthening of the state under the dictatorship of the workers, prior to the emergence of socialism.

This emphasis on the proletariat created a further division between the two camps. The anarchists did not limit their revolutionary forces to the industrial workers, but included peasants, artisans, 'the great rabble of the people' – again rejecting the scientific, class basis of Marxism. In turn, this led to a further split, regarding the road to revolution. Marxist method and organisation primarily involved the formation of a socialist party aiming at political power and control of the state. The anarchists rejected party politics as involving participation in the corrupt capitalist state, and advocated immediate revolution – to be carried out by mass insurrection, not led by politicians.

The anarchist commitment to revolutionary action was dismissed as adventurist and counter-productive by Marxists, while Marxists were accused of being authoritarian and reformist in theory and practice. This represented an early expression of a polemic which has been at the heart of socialist debate ever since, gaining new relevance after the Russian Revolution and the subsequent development of the Soviet Union, and later its satellite states.

Anarchist politics: Terrorism and anarcho-syndicalism

Between the 1880s and our own day, however, the anarchist political experience has largely been one of failure. After the collapse of the First International, anarchism was undermined by its twin weaknesses – ineffectual political violence and impractical idealism. Bakuninist emphasis on direct action led to outbreaks of terrorism, particularly associated with the 1890s.[4] These remained isolated instances which never threatened any government, rather providing an opportunity for widespread arrest of revolutionaries. The other, utopian aspect of anarchism is best represented by the movement's most significant modern ideologue, Kropotkin,[5] whose work concentrated on the nature of post-revolutionary society.

Anarchism needed to become relevant to the everyday experience of workers. In the early years of this century this was attempted through *anarcho-syndicalism*, the most significant practical expression of anarchism. It established the trade union as the vehicle of revolution, and, indeed, the basic organisational structure of post-revolutionary society.[6] This allowed anarchist organisation to develop while remaining outside the hated world of party politics. Sizeable anarcho-syndicalist unions were established, most significantly the French *Confédération Générale du Travail* (CGT) and Spanish *Confederación Nacional del Trabajo* (CNT). These unions aimed at a revolutionary general strike, but again met with harsh government response, leading often to demoralisation. By the First World War, the CGT was reduced to conventional trade union activity.

The anarcho-syndicalist standard was taken up by the CNT, usually considered the most successful and heroic expression of anarcho-syndicalism. Anarchism and anarcho-syndicalism achieved their greatest impact in Spain, and more importantly emerged briefly at the head of a revolutionary situation.[7]

This occurred in 1936, when the Spanish Republic was confronted by a military rising. The anarchists were at the head of the popular response, as the government lost political control. As a result the anarchists found themselves in an unprecedented position of revolutionary leadership, vividly described in George Orwell's *Homage to Catalonia*. There followed a year of political turmoil as the government, aided by the Spanish Communist Party, strove to regain authority, while the anarchists attempted to spread revolution and establish industrial and agricultural cooperatives. The success or failure of these experiments has been hotly debated,[8] and it is difficult to reach a definite conclusion given the chaos of the civil war and the brevity of the experiment. For anarchists, however, the experience served to confirm the fundamentally anti-revolutionary nature of orthodox Marxist and communist practice. The revolution's defeat in Spain saw the disappearance of the last mass anarchist movement.

Notes

(1) For more extensive bibliographies and excellent general histories of anarchism see James Joll, *The Anarchists* (Methuen, 2nd edn. 1979), George Woodcock, *Anarchism*, (Pelican, 2nd edn. 1986), and the more theoretical David Miller, *Anarchism* (J.M. Dent & Sons, 1984). For the texts referred to, see William Godwin, *Enquiry Concerning Political Justice* (1793) ed. I. Kramnick (Penguin, 1976) and Pierre-Joseph Proudhon, *Selected Writings of Pierre-Joseph Proudhon*, ed. S. Edwards (Macmillan, 1970).

(2) Bakunin did not leave a substantial body of written work; the general studies mentioned above provide outlines of his political ideas.

(3) See Marx's *Preface to a Critique of Political Economy* in, among others, K. Marx and F. Engels, *Selected Works* (Lawrence & Wishart, 1968), pp. 181–185.

(4) Joseph Conrad, *The Secret Agent* (1907, repr. Penguin Books, 1990) evokes the twilight world of anarchist conspiracy in turn-of-the-century London.

(5) See G. Woodcock and I. Avakumovic, *The Anarchist Prince: A Biographical Study of Peter Kropotkin* (Schocken Books, 1971).

(6) A clear description of anarcho-syndicalism – and a passionate case for its adoption – is provided by Rudolf Rocker, *Anarcho-Syndicalism* (Secker & Warburg, 1938, repr. Pluto Press, 1989).

(7) An immense amount has been written about Spanish anarchism, creating virtually a sub-literature of its own. For the period prior to the Civil War see Murray Bookchin, *The Spanish Anarchists: The Heroic Years 1868–1936* (Free Life Editions, 1977), an enthusiastic account of the movement up to the Civil War, and for a short and stimulating survey of the developments and recent debates surrounding the years before 1914 see Paul Heywood, 'The Labour Movement in Spain before 1914' in Dick Geary (ed.), *Labour and Socialist Movements in Europe before 1914* (Berg, 1989).

(8) For an accessible work on the Spanish Civil War see Paul Preston, *The Spanish Civil War* (Weidenfeld & Nicholson, 2nd edn. 1989). Favourable studies of the anarchists during the Civil War are Gaston Leval, *Collectives in the Spanish Revolution* (Freedom Press, 1975), Vernon Richards, *Lessons of the Spanish Revolution* (Freedom Press, 1953, repr. 1983) and José Peirats, *Anarchists in the Spanish Revolution* (Freedom Press, repr. 1990).

John Maher lectured in Modern Languages at the University of Salford. His specialised area of research is contemporary Spanish history.

Jeremy Jennings
Syndicalism

Syndicalist ideas, not least concerning the use of the general strike, helped to shape European labour movements in the years before the First World War.

The term syndicalism derives from the French word *syndicat*, which literally translated means nothing more than trade union. However, as a doctrine, syndicalism came to be understood almost exclusively as a form of revolutionary politics advocating the (violent) over-throw of the capitalist system through the tactics of the general strike and a reliance upon working-class labour organisations. Sometimes referred to as anarcho-syndicalism (many of its early adherents were former anarchists), as its name suggests as both a theory and a movement, syndicalism first came to prominence in France.

Origins

The roots of syndicalism lie deep in the political experience of the French working class during the nineteenth century. The repeated defeat of attempts at the insurrectionary seizure of political power and the State machinery led a minority on the Left to conclude that an alternative strategy needed to be developed. This analysis was further confirmed as the century drew to a close. There was a general awareness that the heroic days of revolutionary street-fighting were over – with the development of modern weaponry the advantages of firepower clearly lay with the government – and to this was added a recognition of the futility of what was described as propaganda by the deed (individual terroristic attacks on the members and institutions of the exploiting class). But beyond this, syndicalism reflected a broader disillusionment with the whole world of conventional, bourgeois politics.

In 1870, France's Third Republic came into existence and with this came a democratic regime based upon universal, male, suffrage. Yet the working class remained effectively excluded from power. The Republic, for all its promises about reform and progress, appeared to give the people nothing. Moreover, frequent financial scandals in which many eminent politicians were implicated gave further proof that politics meant corruption. To this was then added the salutary experience of seeing socialists – most notably Alexandre

Millerand – for the first time enter into government, only to turn their backs immediately on their working-class electors. It was governments with socialist representation that used the army to suppress working-class protest and to break strikes. The result was a rejection of the mechanisms of the political process and with that a search for another route to proletarian emancipation. For some, although by no means for all, the *syndicat* or trade union appeared to offer new possibilities.

The pattern of organisation

Trade unions were legalised in France in 1884, but before the First World War they were never able to obtain anything like a mass membership. Official figures, for example, suggest that in 1902 total numbers came to only 614,000. Brought together initially through the *Fédération des Syndicats*, it was in 1895 that the *Confédération Générale du Travail* (CGT) came into existence as an organisation of local, regional and national trade union bodies committed to the use of the general strike. Its structure was to reflect the principles of decentralisation, federalism and autonomy. Spontaneity and an absence of bureaucracy were to be the key themes. In parallel to the CGT there also existed the *Fédération des Bourses du Travail*. *Bourses du travail* were originally intended to be labour-run employment agencies funded by municipal government, but under the leadership of former anarchist Fernand Pelloutier they quickly took on the role of providing a moral, technical and administrative education for the working class, an education that was ultimately aimed at securing the overthrow of the bourgeois capitalist system. Unlike the CGT, which was trade-based, the *bourses du travail* were designed to be a nucleus around which all the workers of a particular area or locality could gather. Furthermore, in the imagined society of the future it was through them that production and consumption would be organised. Here too was to be the centre of working-class social life.

In 1902 both bodies merged, and it was after this that there occurred what appeared to be a wave of (sometimes violent) strike activity and propaganda that struck fear into the hearts of both the government and the bourgeoisie. Crucially at CGT congresses all unions, irrespective of size, had the same number of votes and it was this which in part enabled those committed to revolutionary forms of action and goals to gain the ascendancy. Under the leadership of Victor Griffuelhes, Emile Pouget, Georges Yvetot and Paul Delesalle, the movement in 1906 endorsed what has since been known as the Charter of Amiens, a policy document which defined its goal as the 'complete emancipation' of the workers via 'the expropriation of the capitalist class'. In addition to the publication of an impressive list of pamphlets and newspapers – especially its daily *La Voix du Peuple* – the CGT also tried to get its message across by forging links within the international labour movement. These efforts met with relatively little success and were resolutely opposed by Germany's powerful and reformist unions.

However, the dominance of the revolutionary wing of the movement was never entirely unchallenged. Within the CGT were those who drew inspiration from the British pattern of trade union organisation and who therefore advocated a gradualist approach, seeking to achieve piecemeal reform and the progressive improvement of the material conditions of their members. Amongst these were Auguste Keufer of the printworkers' union. It was to be men like him who after 1909, as the CGT ran into ever greater difficulties, came to have a decisive influence on policy. By 1914 revolutionary *élan* (a favourite syndicalist word) had given way to a grudging acceptance of the harsh realities of a situation in which neither the CGT nor its members were able to overthrow the capitalist system or prevent the outbreak of world war.

Ideology

It was in the first decade of the twentieth century that syndicalism attracted the attention of intellectuals. Moreover it was intellectuals who provided the most articulate expression of syndicalist doctrine. The context here is a complex one, but has its roots in a general shift away from science and rationalism in the final decades of the nineteenth century. Philosophers such as Henri Bergson emphasised the importance of intuition as a form of knowledge, whilst others (probably for the first time) came to appreciate the true power of the unconscious mind. More narrowly, amongst Marxists there was a growing awareness that the orthodoxy of historical materialism was leading to the indefinite postponement of the day of revolution. So too there was a feeling amongst cultural élites that France, and Europe in general, was suffering from a loss of energy. The time seemed right for a new philosophy of action.

In France it was left to Georges Sorel, a retired government engineer of impeccable middle-class credentials, to marry these new intellectual trends to an emerging syndicalist movement ever-eager to go into battle. Sorel's *Reflections on Violence* was published in 1908 and to this day it remains for some a deeply shocking book (amongst its enthusiastic readers was a young Benito Mussolini). The central thesis is that the syndicalist tactic of the general strike has to be seen as a myth capable of engendering the sustained heroic action required from the working class to overthrow the capitalist system and to establish what Sorel describes as a 'sublime morality'. In this, violence plays an integral part, as the proletariat is engaged in an unremitting struggle without possible (or even desirable) compromise. Confrontation and class division were to be welcomed. Acts of kindness were to be repaid by black ingratitude. The goal was to bring 'salvation to the modern world'.

With some justification the leaders of the CGT claimed not to be influenced by Sorel and his friends, but they too were not slow to outline the rudiments of a syndicalist theory. The crucial issue which they and their supporters had to address was the extent to which the *syndicats* were organisations capable of implementing radical change.

The party of work

The crux of the syndicalist case was that the trade union was both an instrument of resistance and also a vehicle of revolution. More than this, by bringing together people who shared a common economic position it was assumed that the *syndicat* embodied both the permanent and real interests of its members. 'The *syndicat*', Pouget wrote, 'groups together those who work against those who live by human exploitation'. It followed, therefore, that the *syndicats* could only be open to members of the working class and that there was no room for such members of the bourgeoisie as doctors and teachers within their ranks. By the same token this implied that by acting within the syndicalist movement the emancipation of the proletariat would be self-emancipation. It was this idea that was given the name direct action.

What did this mean? The first thing to note is that in their discussions of this tactic for the syndicalists the legality or otherwise of a particular action was not of importance. Secondly, the idea was to hit the capitalist where it hurt most: in his pocket. A variety of tactics were considered and employed: go-slows, working to rule, and (most controversial of all) the sabotage and destruction of machinery and property. But centrally the emphasis was to fall upon strike action.

The syndicalists recognised two types of strikes: individual strikes and general strikes. The former were strikes by a group of workers against a single employer, often for a wage increase or a reduction in working hours, but the important innovation from the CGT was that the attainment of these objectives was not seen as an end in itself but as a form of preparation and training for the only battle which ultimately counted: the general strike. On the latter (and despite endless internal debate) the picture was far from clear. Would the workers just stay at home or would there be need for a violent attack on the State? Would all the workers be involved or would it be restricted to key trades and sectors of industry? How long would it last? A few days or a few months? Would it be spontaneous, or would it need leadership from the CGT? No single answer was given. What, however, was beyond doubt – as Emile Pataud and Emile Pouget illustrate in their fantasy *How We Will Make the Revolution* – is that the general strike was not to be the prelude to the revolution but was to constitute the revolution itself. At its end, capitalism would have been abolished and the State would have been destroyed.

The goal of syndicalism

The aim of revolutionary syndicalism was a radical one: nothing less than the wholesale removal of the capitalist system and the bourgeois state and this by a route that bypassed the mechanisms of conventional politics. Capitalism had to go because it was an inefficient and inhumane system of economic exploitation whilst the state – controlled in the interests of the capitalist and the property owner – was integral to its preservation. But what would the syndicalist society of the future look like? Here syndicalists proved remarkably reluctant to let their views be known. The picture that emerged, however, was one of communal ownership and control of the means of production in which human drudgery and suffering would be brought to an end. Rivalry and competition would be replaced by co-operation and mutual aid. The Church would vanish; education would be reformed in the interests of the child; the prisons would be emptied; women would be liberated from domestic slavery. And the army would be abolished.

It was to the last issue that syndicalists devoted much attention. Syndicalists avoided the charge of utopianism by pointing to the fact that the general strike – for example in Russia in 1905 – had already been used as part of a revolutionary struggle. But they were acutely aware that unless the army could at a minimum be neutralised then all hopes of success were illusory. It was for this reason that anti-militarism and anti-patriotism played such an important part in syndicalist thinking. The basic idea was that the workers had to recognise that they had no homeland and that the army – in which they frequently served through conscription – was an instrument in the hands of the bourgeois republic. The doctrine was one of labour internationalism.

The threat of war

With the impending threat of European war this question became ever more pressing. The official policy of the CGT was that in the event of war the workers should refuse to join up and then simultaneously begin a general strike leading to social revolution. To succeed, however, an identical strategy needed to be pursued amongst all the belligerent nations. The French, however, consistently failed to convince their fellow trade unionists of the virtues of this path and then found themselves unable to stop even their own country's headlong rush towards conflict with Germany. In 1914 their bluff was called. Worse still, Léon Jouhaux, the CGT's general secretary from 1909, rallied to the cause of the nation's defence, as did the vast majority of the movement.

After this the CGT effectively split in two. The leadership supported the war effort and with that drifted steadily towards reformism and an endorsement of social democracy. The minority, gravitating around such men as Pierre Monatte, tried to keep the flame of revolutionary syndicalism alive. Sustained by the Russian Revolution of 1917, after the war they rallied to France's new Communist Party, only quickly to find themselves accused (by Trotsky among others) of 'anarcho-syndicalist prejudices'. Refusing to obey the calls for Bolshevisation, they had the privilege of being amongst the very first to fall victim to Stalinist orthodoxy. Expelled from the party there then began the long and lonely attempt (which continued into the 1960s through journals such as *La Révolution prolétarienne*) to preserve the ideology of syndicalism from extinction.

International comparisons

If it was in France that syndicalism as both a revolutionary movement and as a theory reached its height, then it also had adherents elsewhere. In Italy it was organised through the *Unione Sindicale* and attained its high-water mark between 1905 and 1910, after which a general disillusionment set in. Many of its leaders supported Italy's involvement in the First World War, believing that it would revitalise the proletariat. After this the links between syndicalism and nationalism were further developed, leading many of its adherents and theoreticians to transfer their allegiance to Mussolini's fascists. It was this experience that led the Marxist thinker Antonio Gramsci to characterise syndicalism as the reflection of a backward, pre-industrial mentality, appealing predominantly to the poor peasants of the south.

In America too, syndicalism had its supporters, primarily in the form of the Industrial Workers of the World (IWW) or the so-called Wobblies. Founded in 1905, and led by the remarkable 'Big Bill' Heywood, boss of the Western Federation of Miners, at the most it never had more than 60,000 members. It did, however, lead to a series of successful strikes in the years immediately before 1914. The IWW's innovative idea was that of 'one big union': concentrating on the vast numbers of unorganised workers, the intention was to bring 'all the toilers' together, regardless of their trade, into one organisation that would ultimately be able to overthrow capitalism by means of direct, revolutionary action. In truth, the Wobblies were never able to compete with the powerful and reformist American Federation of Labour led by Samuel Gompers and in any case the potential for revolutionary change in the USA was severely limited.

British syndicalism

Britain also was not entirely immune from the syndicalist virus. Here the key figure was former dockers' leader Tom Mann who, on returning from Australia in 1910 (stopping off in Paris to meet syndicalist leaders), established the Industrial Syndicalist Education League complete with its own journal, *The Industrial Syndicalist*. As in America, in organisational terms the emphasis fell on industrial unionism and the attempt to overcome sectionalism within the working class, but the methods to be employed were those of the French: anti-parliamentary direct action. The year 1912 saw the publication of *The Miners' Next Step* by the 'Unofficial Reform Committee' in the South Wales coalfield, a document seemingly embracing the syndicalist message of decentralised and non-bureaucratic workers' control, and this was accompanied by a wave of industrial unrest, most notably in transport, engineering and building. Again 1914 brought such militancy to a close. After the war the growth of the Labour Party and the continued dominance of the TUC left the syndicalists little room for advance. Many found their way into the Shop Stewards' Movement.

It was, therefore, only in Spain that revolutionary syndicalism survived in any strength after 1918. Founded in 1910, the *Confederación Nacional de Trabajo* (CNT) recruited mainly from the industrial workers of Catalonia and the peasants of Andalucia, obtaining perhaps as many as one million members. Agitation and strikes continued throughout the 1920s and when what was already virtually civil war was turned into actual civil war in 1936, the CNT found itself in control of wide areas of Spain. In Barcelona – as George Orwell testified in *Homage to Catalonia* – syndicalist ideas were begun to be put into practice, and with some success. The end result, however, was military defeat at the hands of Franco's fascists and betrayal by the communists. Those who survived were forced into exile.

Conclusion

For all its intellectual vibrancy and commitment to action the record of syndicalism in the twentieth century has been one of defeat and rejection. On the Left its supporters were always a minority. However it has never entirely gone away, and today perhaps there is room for a comeback. The collapse of the USSR (and the discredit of Soviet-style communism) combined with a broader shift away from State socialism means that if the Left is to survive it needs a new direction. For those not content with social democracy, syndicalism might offer some inspiration.

Further Reading

Brissenden, P.F. *The Launching of the Industrial Workers of the World* (Haskell, 1971).

Holton, B. *British Syndicalism 1900–14* (Pluto Press, 1976).

Jennings, J. *Syndicalism in France: A History of Ideas* (Macmillan, 1990).

Milner, S. *French Syndicalism and the International Labour Movement 1900–14* (Berg, 1991).

Ridley, F.F. *Revolutionary Syndicalism in France* (Cambridge University Press, 1970).

Roberts, D.L. *The Syndicalist Tradition in Italian Fascism* (University of North Carolina).

Thorpe, W. *'The Workers Themselves': Revolutionary Syndicalism and International Labour 1913–23* (Kluwer Academic Publishers, 1989).

Jeremy Jennings is Senior Lecturer in the Department of Political Theory and Government at the University of Swansea.

Ian Porter and Ian D. Armour
Men Without a Fatherland?
The SPD in Imperial Germany

Introduction

There was a paradox about the Social Democratic Party of Germany (after 1891 *Sozialdemokratische Partei Deutschlands*, or SPD) in the imperial period. Persecuted under Bismarck, the SPD nevertheless became the fastest growing and, by 1912, the largest party in the imperial parliament or Reichstag. The Social Democrats achieved this, moreover, despite the continuing hostility of the political establishment. From Bismarck, who denounced them as 'men without a fatherland', to the Emperor William II, for whom every socialist was an 'enemy of the Reich', the Social Democrats were seen as a threat to the existing order, with whom no compromise was possible.[1]

Both the SPD's growing electoral strength, and the fear it inspired, were due to a real confusion as to whether the Party was revolutionary or reformist, a question which has tended to colour historical scholarship ever since. Recent research, however, suggests that this distinction is a non-issue. The SPD was never quite one thing or the other. Of more interest to historians, at the moment, is the question of how far the party genuinely represented working-class opinion in Germany. There were many varieties of working-class experience, depending on region, religious background and ethnic character. The history of the SPD cannot be equated with that of the whole of the German working classes.[2]

Beginnings of policial organisation 1848–71

Despite this, the SPD was still the most prominent working-class organisation throughout the imperial period. It had its roots in the various workers' associations which sprang up in the 1840s, at a time when economic conditions made the life of the traditional artisan class particularly precarious. It was they, rather than the new factory workers, who formed the first self-help and educational associations, just as it was discontented and impoverished artisans, not factory workers, who manned the barricades in the 1848 revolutions in Germany.

Repressed in 1848, workers' associations began to emerge once again in the 1850s in those German states where the political climate permitted it. In March 1863 a number of different groups combined to form the General German Workers' Association (*Allgemeiner deutscher Arbeiterverein*, or ADAV) in Leipzig, under a programme drawn up by Ferdinand Lassalle.

Lassalle (1825–64) was a radical lawyer whose thinking on social issues had been decisively shaped by the experiences of 1848. The liberal failure effectively to resist Bismarck's conservative government in Prussia, after 1862, also confirmed Lassalle in his conviction that the working class must have its own political party. Lassalle, like Marx and Engels, believed in the redistribution of wealth, which in turn involved the abolition of private property and capital. Unlike the Marxists, however, Lassallean socialists also believed that the state had a positive role to play in engineering social change, if only because the voting power of the masses, once enfranchised, would force it to do so. The ADAV accordingly was committed to manhood suffrage as the quickest route to social democracy.

The 1860s also saw the emergence of a more explicitly Marxist working-class party, led by August Bebel (1848–1913) and Wilhelm Liebknecht (1826–1900). Both men were active initially as radical democrats, but gradually became convinced, like Lassalle, that working-class interests could only be represented by a working-class party. At Eisenach, in August 1869, Bebel and Liebknecht founded the Social Democratic Workers' Party (*Sozialdemokratische Arbeiterpartei*, or SDAP). Liebknecht in particular was much influenced by the thinking of his friend, Marx, and the new party openly proclaimed its commitment to 'the abolition of all class rule', and the replacement of the wage system by a co-operative mode of production.[3] The SDAP was also in favour of manhood suffrage, which gave it some common ground with the ADAV.

The merger of 1875 and the anti-socialist period 1878–90

Membership of both parties remained low: as late as 1875 the SDAP had only 9,000 members, the ADAV 15,000. Apart from the advantage of solidarity, a number of other factors encouraged their merger in the 1870s. The two parties had differed over how to achieve German unification: Lassalle and his successors accepted the need for Prussian leadership, while the SDAP opposed the idea of unification by force. After Bismarck forcibly founded the German Empire in 1871 this was no longer a problem. More pressing was the need to defend workers' interests in the face of government hostility, and the worsening economic situation following the stock market crash of 1873.

At Gotha in May 1875, both sides agreed on a common programme, calling for universal suffrage, state-funded education, a national, graduated income tax, rather than indirect raxes which penalised the poor, and legislation 'to protect the lives and health of workers'.[4] Liebknecht's views prevailed over Lassalle's, in that the working class was seen as opposed to all other classes. The new party named itself the Socialist Workers' Party of Germany (*Sozialistische Arbeiterpartei Deutschlands*).

The Marxist tone of the Gotha programme confirmed Bismarck in his prejudice against the socialists, an animosity which went back to their opposition to continued war against republican France in 1870, and their sympathy for the Paris Commune of 1871. Bismarck was also alarmed at the gains the socialists made in the Reichstag election of 1877, with nearly half a million votes and thirteen seats. In 1878, two separate assassination attempts against the Emperor William I, neither connected with the Socialist Workers' Party, gave Bismarck the pretext he needed for cracking down on it.[5] After fresh elections to manufacture a majority for anti-socialist legislation, the Chancellor secured approval for a 'Law against the Dangerous Activities of Social Democracy' in October 1878.

The Anti-Socialist Law remained in force until 1890. Under its provisions any 'Social Democratic, Socialistic, or Communist' organisations, including associated trades unions, deemed by the government to be seeking 'to overthrow the existing political and social order', were declared illegal. So were public meetings and publications supposed to be serving the same purpose. The Socialist Workers' Party itself was not banned, and could still put up candidates at national and local elections, but all the normal methods of political campaigning, such as newspapers, pamphleting, and mass rallies, were now impossible. Some underground newspapers were successfuly launched after 1878, notably the Zürich-based *Sozialdemokrat*, but party members discovered taking part in such illegal activities could be evicted from their homes and were frequently imprisoned.[6]

Despite these restrictions, the Socialist Workers' Party continued to make remarkable progress at the polls. In the elections of 1884 it received over half a million votes. By 1890, in the last election held under the Anti-Socialist Law, almost one and a half million people voted for the party, which won thirty-five seats in the Reichstag. Bismarck had tried to win over the working-class vote by introducing the first social security legislation, offering a rudimentary form of health, accident and old age insurance. Welcome though this was, none of it affected the growing identification of working-class voters with the only party which explicitly claimed to represent their interest, and which by now already had 19.7% of the vote.

The reasons for this rise are still a matter of debate. Undoubtedly one factor was that the party organisation, even under the Anti-Socialist Law, offered its members what one historian has called an 'alternative culture'.[7] The party ran its own educational courses, libraries, sports clubs, even choral societies. Festivals and parades such as May Day were important social and family events as well as political demonstrations, and such solidarity bred loyalty at the polling booths.

At the same time it must be remembered that social democratic activity was not the only working-class culture on offer. With some encouragement from the government, rival Catholic and Protestant working men's clubs and unions emerged. The large numbers of migrant Polish workers, in industrial areas like the Ruhr, also had their own organisations. Social Democracy was simply the most visible of a variety of such organisations.

The struggle for acceptance 1890–1914

Bismarck's fall was a direct consequence of his struggle with the young Emperor William II (1888–1918) over the introduction of a more rigorous, and permanent, law against socialism. The Chancellor, faced with the probable rejection of such legislation by the Reichstag, was so obsessed with the socialist threat that he contemplated dispensing with parliamentary rule. William II, however, shrank from taking such a step, and after dismissing Bismarck simply let the Anti-Socialist Law expire.

This nevertheless did not mean a change in the official attitude. William II was if anything even more given to hysterical, and highly public, denunciations of all socialist activity as subversive. The Emperor's conviction, derived from Bismarck, was that socialists simply could not be good Germans, and continued to set the tone for the pre-1914 period. It ensured that working-class people still felt stigmatised and excluded from society. In practical terms it posed problems for any government seeking to govern with a Reichstag majority, since the number of working-class representatives there was growing all the time.

The party took stock of the situation at its Erfurt conference in 1891, when it renamed itself the Social Democratic Party of Germany, the name by which it has been known ever since. To some extent the difficulties the SPD experienced in gaining acceptance, after 1890, were of its own making. On a practical level, after years of persecution, the last thing Social Democrats wanted was confrontation, and this was reflected in their preoccupation with largely bread-and-butter issues such as the length of the working day, wages, and housing. On a theoretical level, however, Erfurt reiterated the commitment to achieving common ownership of the means of production. Many SPD politicans continued to employ a militant jargon of class struggle which seemed to imply a determination to effect change by violent means. It is not surprising, then, that confusion persisted as to what Social Democracy's aims really were.

This debate about aims was effectively won by the advocates of gradual reform, rather than revolution, long before 1914. It was increasingly clear to many party members that the only practical way of satisfying 'the most immediate needs of the people' was by working within the system. Just as clearly, doing so would amount to a 'gradual socialisation' of Germany itself.[8] Late in the 1890s reformism received a theoretical justification, when Eduard Bernstein argued that German society was not conforming to the Marxist model of ever sharpening class conflict. Although the condition of the working class remained deplorable, there had been a relative improvement in its standard of living, due to the rapid expansion of the German economy.

The most powerful impetus toward moderation was the attitude taken by Social Democratic trade unions. Legalised again in 1890, they had grown swiftly, with a new General Commission of Trade Unions. Union activists made clear their impatience with the theoretical side of socialism, and concentrated instead on the practical problems confronting members. They did much to improve conditions, negotiating places for working-class representatives on housing committees and other local government bodies.

Despite all these signs of the SPD's essential moderation, the Emperor and his ministers continued to regard it as beyond the pale, and their abhorrence was only deepened by the SPD's steady increase in the polls. It received two million votes in 1898; three million in 1903; and four and a quarter million in 1912, with 110 seats out of 397 in the Reichstag. This made the SPD the largest single party, and yet no government would even contemplate governing with Social Democratic support.

War and revolution 1914–18

The outbreak of war in Europe demonstrated just how groundless the German establishment's fear of Social Democratic revolution really was. Faced with what they sincerely believed was an unprovoked attack on Germany by the most reactionary regime in Europe, tsarist Russia, the SPD voted unanimously in favour of the government's war credits. The government had been desperately anxious for Russia to appear the aggressor, for it knew how vital Social Democratic support would be in mobilising the German working class for war. And so it proved. Assured by the party leadership

masters, were divided between France and Germany. However, the assumption that the maintenance of trading relationships was of paramount importance was not shared by all capitalists. It was much stronger in Great Britain, whose position had been established largely through free trade, than in Prussia which had always depended on conquest for access to raw materials and on tariffs for protection of nascent industries.

Even within individual countries, opinions varied from one section of the economy to another. Merchants and financiers feared war more than industrialists; a trading city, like Hamburg, valued free trade more than Berlin. Large-scale industrialists on the continent were increasingly likely to be linked to the state, which reduced their interest in private clients in other European countries. Furthermore, some heavy industries – Krupps in Germany, Schneider in France – knew that much of their production was consumed by the military. Capitalists of the mid-nineteenth century had often been robustly independent and deeply sceptical of projects advanced by the aristocrats who dominated politics and the military. Eventually, such people began to intermarry with the aristocracy, and their children became associated with aristocratic or pseudo-aristocratic institutions; sometimes they seem to have adopted extreme parodies of what they imagined to be aristocratic values. The German army became more authoritarian, and hierarchical in manner as it recruited larger numbers of bourgeois officers. Members of business dynasties, such as the Kenricks of Birmingham, eventually became more interested in politics than in the management of their own enterprises.

But what of the great public enthusiasm that greeted war in 1914? What of the cheering crowds and the young men queuing outside the recruiting offices? In fact assumptions about the popular mood of 1914 are open to the same questions that are always raised about the assessment of public opinion. A.J.P. Taylor suggested that crowds might have cheered just as loudly if it had been announced that 'war had not been declared'. The most detailed survey of public opinion in France in 1914 suggests that war was greeted with much foreboding: 'It is the death knell of our boys' said one Frenchman when he heard the bells being rung to announce mobilisation. Furthermore, the crowds who cheered were not representative samples of any country's population. Peasants were much less enthusiastic about the war than city dwellers. Many peasants had a very limited sense of loyalty to the nation which was now demanding their blood, and they were particularly hostile to a war that began when the harvest was due to be collected. In Russia, two million peasants got married and, thereby, made themselves ineligible for military service, in August 1914.

Even in the cities' support for the war was not uniform. The cheering crowds were to be found in the commercial and administrative city centres not in the outer industrial areas. The men in these crowds wore collars and ties and trilby hats not scarves and cloth caps. Knowing what the working classes themselves thought of the war is awkward. Some historians have suggested that the workers had been seduced from their class loyalty and international solidarity by 'social imperialist' propaganda. Social imperialism was seen to have been the means by which ruling classes sought to incite chauvinist dislike of national rivals as a means to prevent revolutionary agitation. This interpretation runs into a number of difficulties. It does not work at all for Austria-Hungary where 'imperial socialism' was practised as the Emperor extended the franchise in the hope that class based labour parties might undercut the nationalist movements that were threatening the unity of the state. Social imperialism also meant something very different in other European countries. In England, Empire was linked with real increase in living standards: cheap imports of cocoa and tea flooded in, and the survival of the Lancashire cotton industry was secured by the extinction of the Indian one. In Germany, by contrast, imperial expansion brought few material benefits to the German working class, or anyone else for that matter; here social imperialism was seen as offering primarily psychological satisfactions. In France imperialism did not even have much of a psychological dimension; colonial expansion was undertaken by an isolated group of civil servants and soldiers and barely noticed by the country as a whole.

Even if 'social imperialism' is loosely defined to mean popular nationalist chauvinism there is not much evidence that it had an effect on the working classes. Many historians assumed that there must have been a link between the nationalist propaganda directed at workers and the fact that such workers turned away from revolutionary agitation. In fact, there were other reasons why workers accepted their lot under capitalism. Furthermore, people can be remarkably impervious to the crudest propaganda (a survey conducted in Britain during the early 1980s showed that, not only were most readers of the *Sun* Labour voters, but that 28% of them believed the *Sun* to be a Labour paper).

If social imperialism had little impact on the working classes, it did have an effect on two other social groups. The first of these was the lower middle class. It has been suggested above that the numbers of shop assistants, clerks and menial white-collar employees were increasing in all industrialised countries in the early twentieth century. These groups were particularly vulnerable to nationalist propaganda, even if such propaganda was not primarily aimed at them. They worked in city centres, they were literate and likely to read publications produced by their social betters. They also aspired to share a culture with those betters. The sense of frustration and boredom that these groups often felt was particularly likely to manifest itself in military interests. Warfare was associated with the upper classes, it had often provided a means of social mobility. War seemed to offer ledger clerks and office boys an escape from the tedium and humiliation of their daily life. It was this that accounted for the sense of joy that sometimes seemed to accompany the beginnings of wartime mobilisation. In Great Britain, the only country where all troops were volunteers rather than conscripts, the 'pals' battalions' of early volunteers were largely made up of shop assistants and clerks.

The other class that was influenced by social imperialism was the ruling class. It is often assumed that the members of the ruling class were cold-blooded and omnipotent manipulators. In reality, popular nationalism acquired a momentum of its own that often made it difficult for its originators to control. Furthermore rulers, especially in Germany and Austria-Hungary, often believed that there was a revolutionary threat within their own countries, even if this was not the case, and sometimes came to believe that advancing forward into war was the only way to defuse this threat. Fears of social or national revolution tied in with broader fears that haunted all European rulers in 1914. Every nation had reason to believe it was weak. Britain ruled over an extensive but vulnerable Empire: prescient Englishmen had already noted the relative economic decline that would make the Empire hard to defend. Austria-Hungary had even greater problems of 'imperial over-reach'. Germany was encircled by potentially hostile powers. The French knew that Germany was a more advanced industrial power, and the Russians knew that almost every power was more advanced. Sometimes, the rich and powerful had particular reasons to be fearful. The Prussian Junkers had estates on the eastern frontier and dreaded a Russian advance. The iron-masters of Eastern France had similar fears for their factories in the event of German invasion. Fear rather than greed was the dominant emotion of August 1914 and, in some sense, everyone had reason to believe that they were acting in self-defence.

Norman Stone
The Habsburg Monarchy: Multiethnic Anachronism?

In this analysis of the Habsburg Monarchy Norman Stone evokes the complex ethnic, religious, cultural and linguistic character of the Austro-Hungarian Empire.

The Habsburg Monarchy is the most difficult thing to discuss. I myself was reminded of the extraordinary difficulty of the subject and its extraordinary charm because on Christmas Eve 1989, the *Daily Telegraph* asked me if I would go and do a report in Romania. You arrive in a place like Transylvania and you are dealing with little towns and villages which are recognisably our neck of the woods. They are Protestant, they are quite clean and well organised. The churches look like Lutheran churches – some of the population is Lutheran, some Calvinistic, some Catholic and there is a big Romanian Orthodox element.

Subsequently I found myself at a conference in Prague. I do advise you to go to Prague. One of the very good things about Communism is that although places get dynamited, as in Bucharest, to build avenues to such things as the victory of socialism, they are usually quite good, partly by neglect and partly by policy, at keeping together the centres of towns. And the result is that a place like Prague has been kept together. It may be in a crumbling state, but kept together and only really waiting for a lick of paint to be restored as a perfect central European city.

It is a tremendously varied place which is why I think virtually all historians would shy away from it. If I think about the sheer problem of describing the Habsburg Empire I can see why it is. There aren't many good books on the subject because once you go beyond the descriptive anecdotal level you really are into a nightmare of historiography – you're describing so many different things. You enter Austria at Bregenz on the shores of Lake Constance – a very Austrian town and it gets more Austrian in the twee sense as you go into the Alps across Salzburg, then you go into Bohemia and discover a perfectly modern country which, in the 1930s, had the same standard of living as Belgium and was well and truly on the European industrial map. You go into Moravia which is all prosperous agriculture; you come into Slovakia which is a very heavily Catholic country and it is the complete heart of central

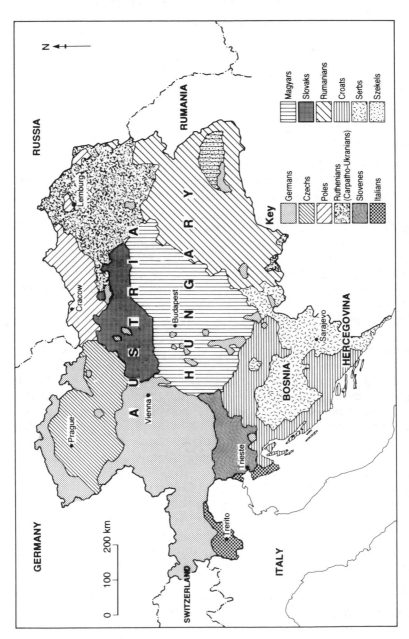

The multiethnic composition of the Austrian-Hungarian Empire

Europe – little old ladies dressed in black, driving geese across muddy streets, quite a lot of drunkenness, peasant costumes which vary from village to village. From there into the sprawling Polish part, Galicia, where part of it, Cracow, is western in the Catholic central European sense; and there are an awful lot of Baroque churches. Then on to what was the eastern part of the former Austro-Hungarian empire which until recently was part of the Soviet Union, where there is the same sort of thing in a rather more elegant style and you discover that the population ceases to be Polish and suddenly becomes Ukrainian.

I stress all this because it makes the subject very difficult to deal with. However, I want to put it to you that the outcome of all this is actually so interesting in the twentieth century for the subject to be well worth looking at and starting over with. Only perhaps not quite in the spirit in which it has been approached hitherto.

Europe's treasure vault

Let me start off simply by talking of the world of Vienna and Budapest in 1900. You look at the sort of people who are talking, writing, building, painting and composing in Vienna in 1900 and you have something of the picture. I do not understand why it should be so, but it simply is a fact that Vienna in the later 1890s, though the capital of an empire which was not in good shape at all and which had suffered from terrible operatic politics, is nevertheless the place where they invent things. There is Freud, of whom I'm not a great fan. Freud seems to me to have been a narcissus figure who grew older and grumpier and said some very silly things. However, he obviously hit on a truth which ran right through Europe at the time and particularly in the 1920s and 1930s. Also incidentally and again in ways which cannot be translated into English, rather like Kafka, he is a very funny writer because he makes fun of words as he uses them, sending them up; a particularly untranslatable style of humour but which, nonetheless, I have to call attention to. There is Wittgenstein the philosopher and Schoenberg the composer. The ideas, innovations and experiments of these people are very influential throughout western culture through most of the twentieth century. I suppose it is fair to say the man who invented the tower block is Viennese. If you are looking at Vienna in 1900 you will see these sprawling great semi-slums, and conclude we must start planning towns. Now the English have got their answer in town planning which is garden suburbs like Letchworth. In Vienna instead they conclude we must use new materials, we must build to a satisfactory height, we can put people in that way into zones which are free of factories and pollution and we can organise transport. These buildings do not have much decoration, but they remake cities on the basis of the tower block. The man responsible is a Viennese architect, Otto Wagner. It is wrong to think of tower block estates as being an American idea as they subsequently appeared to be. These ideas came from central Europe, specifically from Vienna. Now I stress this simply to say that before 1914 central Europe is doing something very remarkable.

In the sixteenth century Hungarian existed as a European language as did Czech. There were criss-crossings on the Protestant international network between Edinburgh, Eastern Hungary and Bohemia. In the seventeenth century Hungary and Bohemia were affected by the Catholic counter-Reformation, or in the case of Transylvania, relapsed into a kind of provinciality. In all cases the language was replaced by German, which became the language to speak, whilst Latin became the language to some extent in legal matters. Now what do you do at the end of the eighteenth century? Somebody called Herder in Germany begins to emphasise the importance for the development of the individual of his national self-identification. That means a language. The French Revolution gives a further fillip to this development. The problem for the Hungarians is that by then their language had really declined to being a peasant dialect. You have got fifteen words for cucumber, depending on its state of decay. You have otherwise certain obvious verbs expressing certain rudimentary physical actions. There are some dusty old books from which you can get some kind of archaic expressions, but what you do in these circumstances is sit down and invent a language.

I find this rather dangerous, but after all, it has been done in our century by Hebrew, which had, in effect, to be reinvented and it is still being done by the Irish. I am told by people who know about these things that Irish can only really be understood if your English is very good because its enemies would call it a fake language and its friends would say it is a language which had to be invented for the sake of self-identification. Hungarian has a bit of that quality, so does Czech. You have to go along and take the Germanic ways of doing things – you do not use them directly but you translate these Germanic compounds bit by bit into your own native language so that the Germanic words which give you such literal ideas as trouser carriers for braces get translated into trouser and carrier, or for postman letter and carrier, for telephone, distant speaker. All of these things get translated and with the abstractions in German it is much worse. Now the result is that when these people write prose they are very often writing a version of German. It is less so nowadays but it is still something which makes books on the Habsburg Monarchy sometimes difficult to follow.

There is a famous instance of this which is still on the A-level lists by a very worthy man, who was a sort of left liberal who thought that the way the Hungarians treated their minority peoples was a disgrace, as to a large extent it often was. He did not like the First World War – he would rather have been neutral – admired the West, England in particular and was a good sociologist. He wrote a very good book in the United States which is called *The Dissolution of the Habsburg Monarchy*. Probably, as A.J.P. Taylor remarked at the end of his bibliography, this book would be enormously valuable if anyone could read it.

The complications do not stop there. What is Ukrainian? In north-eastern Hungary they spoke one sort of Ukrainian. Meanwhile there are three sorts of Ukrainian spoken in the north-eastern chunk of what was the Habsburg Monarchy. It becomes fathomlessly complex. Then you get into Transylvania where there are Germans, Hungarians, Romanians. Meanwhile in the south Slav area of the former empire there are Croats and Slovenes, with smatterings of Bulgarians and Armenians. The origins of the conductor Herbert von Karajan lie in Armenia. In the eighteenth century his family, trading across the Black Sea with Romania in Turkish times, would latch on to a trade route going through Bulgaria towards Dalmatia. In the course of the eighteenth century the Habsburgs built up Trieste and an energetic Karajan would go up the coast to Trieste and there he would rub shoulders with merchants with names like Calvocoressi and Mavrocordato. These are Italian-Greek names which come from what was a Greek island in Turkey, settled by Italians who tacked a Greek bit on to the end of their name, came to Trieste, went to Vienna, made a bit of money and in the course of time came to London where they put their children through public schools. There is now a significant section in London which has got this mixture of Greek and Italian names.

I stress all of these things because I want to say that it is very, very difficult to talk about the Habsburg Monarchy as any kind of unity. For instance, when Austro-Hungary went to war in 1914, mobilisation happened in 15 languages, including Yiddish. Now you can imagine what a nightmare it is running that kind of Army. The Austro-Hungarian Army had to have all kinds of strange emergency solutions to problems. For instance, in 1915 a Slovak regiment which was recruited partly from Hungarians, partly from Germans, partly from Slovaks, and partly from Ruthenes had to be commanded in English because the soldiers had learned that language with a view to emigrating and the officers had learnt it at school. They had no other common language.

Language and nationalism

All of this defies rational analysis, and certainly it defies any kind of Whig interpretation. You cannot talk about the history of the Habsburg Monarchy as any kind of unity stretching back to the Middle Ages as you could do with English history and to some extent with French. You're dealing with a problem of such diversity that it resists even the unification of the historical textbook. This is complicated further by the fact that German was the dominant language of the Habsburg Monarchy. A lot of the other languages consequently took on the same character as German. People like the Hungarians, in the nineteenth century, reasserted themselves and their national identity, but they had to some extent to re-invent the language in the process.

Equally remarkable are developments in Budapest. We do not know Budapest in this country at all well, nor have we had much cause to do so since it has been relatively isolated since 1945. But if you go to Budapest you can see what central Europe is all about. This is a city with medieval origins. In the eighteenth century, since Hungary was very much a colony of the Habsburg Empire, Budapest was not particularly distinguished, whereas in Vienna you find great big noble piles – about six Lobkovitz palaces, seven Kinski palaces and 18 Schwarzenberg palaces – each assuming a large part of the GNP. You do not find that in Buda which is the Buda side of Budapest on the right bank of the river. What you find after 1870 is an extraordinary nineteenth-century city. It is well planned and developed as a civilisation. Budapest grew in a generation from 150,000 to being a city of two million inhabitants, becoming one of the great world cities. Now Hungarian politics before 1914 were almost grotesque and operatic. Hungary herself appears to be rather an artifical country with a particular history of political development. Here is a parliament built in 1904 which is only representative of about 5% of the population, chosen quite literally on the basis of people who had ancestors who were on the electoral roll in the sixteenth century and whose names ended in a combination of 'y' and 'i' – the noble class. Look at the noble class and what does it consist of? Half the people who were in the noble class have roughly the equivalent of a heavily mortgaged apple tree. The politics of the place appear to be almost grotesque again insofar as there are lots of parties which split and re-split, there is a Nationalist Party which defies the Habsburgs and a Liberal Party which does not like the Habsburgs but plays along. There are some very grand noble names where the people own a great deal of money and there is an almost unmanageable atmosphere in the politics of the place. Not only that but Hungary consisted of half or, by some accounts, over half of non-Hungarian speakers; Transylvania, in particular, being difficult but also Croatia.

You might look at a place like this and regard it with the eyes of President Woodrow Wilson and say, 'What a nightmare, Hungary must be knocked down to size and turned into a national state.' On the other side you can look at it and greatly respect what was actually achieved in the place by 1900. There was the music and literature and science.

This is despite the fact that Hungary was a poor country with not very much in the way of natural resources which has come up from almost nothing in the middle of the nineteenth century and politically is in rather a bad way. It is conundrums such as these which arouse interest in the Habsburg Monarchy. Culturally it has been enormously rich since the eighteenth century.

Part of this cultural richness is not so much the fact of the 15 different languages spoken in the empire. But the reawakening of national identity in the nineteenth century was certainly a factor and obviously something to do with the kind of musical enthusiasm and drive which would go into the making of Dvořák or Bartók. Bartók, for instance, went round Romania and Transylvania with very primitive recording equipment, listening to folk songs and then orchestrating them. The object was to provide, through the songs of the peasants, the locus for a national cultural identity.

The cement of the empire

The extraordinary thing is the way in which this strange empire was knitted together. It has got three very important religious strands in it which really are the making of the place. You see the great romantic glossy side of Vienna in 1900. It looks like the great counter-Reformation monarchy, it has terribly cumbersome old-fashioned Spanish rituals, its palaces go on for miles, there are endless Baroque churches and it looks as if it was what it claimed to be, the great Catholic monarchy. But behind it is something else, something that goes back to the Reformation of the sixteenth and seventeenth centuries. Protestantism had a continuing effect on the various parts of the Habsburg Monarchy. As late as 1900 you will find in Transylvania that the Calvinists are about 90% literate, the Lutherans 60% literate, the Catholics 35% literate and the Orthodox 10% literate. In other words the Reformation continued to affect the social geography of the Habsburg Monarchy. There is also a very important Jewish element and when you look at Vienna with its Jewish population of about 10%, Budapest where it reached 25% or Prague where it was about 15% or Trieste were it was about 20%, you can see a specifically Jewish element in the Habsburg Monarchy

The Balkans, 1878–1908

the 1870s. Rebellion broke out in Bosnia and Hercegovina in 1875. The Serbs launched a war against the Turks in 1876, with the help of some Bulgarian detachments. This was the background for the Bulgarian uprising of April 1876. Building on a tradition of successful banditry, Bulgarian intellectuals had formed a number of revolutionary groups in the country. These had come together in 1870 to form a Bulgarian Revolutionary Central Committee, which coordinated the rebellion. Aiming to exploit the peasants' rising expectations of land and reduced taxation and their resentment of administrative abuses by local officials, they produced a revolt in three mountain towns. This was a disaster, with the mass of the peasantry refusing to follow the generally middle-class activists. If the Turkish soldiery had behaved sensibly, the incident would have been a mere footnote in history. However, the brutal manner in which they suppressed the revolt and their revengeful massacre of the population, with probably around 15,000 being killed, led to a European-wide furore. These atrocities had forced the Bulgarian issue on to the European stage, and the great powers felt obliged to intervene to prevent a repetition.

Russia and the Bulgarian Question

Russia's policy towards the Balkans had long been far from clear or consistent. Offical policy as defined by the Tsar and his Foreign Minister was often contradicted by the semi-independent Asiatic Department of the Ministry of Foreign Affairs, which tended to follow its own distinctive line of policy and action. Unoffical action by leading military figures and pressures from public opinion and the nationalistic wing of the press further muddied the waters.

In the 1830s and 1840s, the arch-conservative Nicholas I, in his role as the armed policeman of Europe, was intensely suspicious of any national movement threatening to upset the established order. He went to war against the Turks in 1828, but only the Greeks and not the Bulgarians had benefited directly from that. Thereafter, he resumed his support for the preservation of the Ottoman Empire. Continued Turkish decline endangered Russia's vital interests. In particular, Russia's military and developing commerical interests demanded free passage for her ships from the warm-water ports in the Black Sea through the Straits of Constantinople to the Mediterranean. It was Russia's efforts to counter growing French and British influence in Constantinople, and her occupation of the Danubian Principalities to provide a platform for overland access to the Straits that led to the Crimean War. This resulted in military disaster and humiliation for Russia. The peace congress in Paris in 1856 deeply wounded Russia's national pride and self-interest by forcing territorial concessions which separated her firmly from the Straits, and by insisting on the demilitarisation of the Black Sea.

The new Tsar, Alexander II, and his foreign minister, Gorchakov, were far from being adventurers. International caution was needed in order to reorganise Russia internally and to recover the economic strength needed to support an active foreign policy. With the continued weakening of the Turks' control over the Balkan section of their Empire, there was a real threat that Austria would advance to extend her influence over the whole peninsula from her existing base in the north. With a multi-national empire including many Slavs, the Austrians could not but be alarmed at the possible knock-on effect on their subjects of yet more independent Slav states, particularly if under Russian tutelage. Their attempted expansion in this area was thus essentially defensive in motivation. To counter the Austrians, deeply mistrusted after their hostile neutrality during the Crimean War, Alexander II and Gorchakov initially co-operated with France. Restraint turned into revenge when Russia supported the new Germany in her victorious war against the Habsburgs in 1866. The Russians cheered on the Germans when they humiliated France in 1870. They took advantage of France's confusion to reclaim the right to maintain a Black Sea fleet and to send it through the Straits into the Mediterranean. The Russians themselves extended their Empire into Central Asia in the 1860s and 1870s, thereby causing alarm in British India. Russia's rehabilitation as a great power and the restoration of her former sense of security seemed to be assured in 1872 when the Three Emperors' League revived the conservative Austro-German-Russian alliance which had traditionally made her western frontiers secure and enforced obedient subordination on lesser nationalities.

The rise of Russian nationalism

However, the turbulent nationalism of the Balkans was no longer to be so easily controlled. Nor were the internal forces which contributed to the unofficial side of Russia's foreign policy. This was rooted in a rising tide of Russian nationalism, based on a conviction of Russia's uniqueness and superiority. The belief that Moscow was the Third Rome had been established as early as the fifteenth century, after the fall of Constantinople to Islam. Russian Orthodoxy was seen as the only true Christianity, offering the hope of salvation to the rest of mankind. As the Third Rome, Russia had the right and duty to defend fellow Orthodox elsewhere, a claim which had contributed to the outbreak of the Crimean War. Russian nationalists were also very conscious that they were Slavs, inherently different from and spiritually superior to their Western rivals.

A feeling of Slav brotherhood had developed by the 1860s into a strident Panslav nationalism which asserted Russia's dominant position in the Slav world. The popular outburst against the Polish rebels in 1863, and the savagery with which they were suppressed, demonstrated this point with brutal clarity.

The Foreign Ministry's Asiatic Department contained many officials of Panslav sympathies who did not feel themselves to be bound by the constraints of official policies. Consuls throughout the Balkans encouraged fellow Slavs to organise and rise against Turkish or Austrian overlordship. Raevskii, chaplain at the Russian Embassy in Vienna, was especially active in developing such contacts and in reviling the Austrians. A leading proponent of this tendency, Count Ignatiev, became ambassador in Constantinople in 1864.

The Hercegovinian revolt in 1875 thus provided ample scope for confusion in Russia's response. When the Serbs, fellow Slavs and co-religionists, seemed to be on the point of attacking the Turks in 1876, the unofficial elements in Russia could no longer be restrained. Nationalistic journalists like M.N. Katkov raised the temperature to fever pitch, and money poured in to support an army of volunteers to aid Serbia. Command was taken by General M.G. Cherniaev, the so-called 'Lion of Tashkent' famous for his role in Russia's recent victories in Central Asia. Fired by an intense hatred of the Tsar and the War Minister, D.A. Miliutin, this flamboyant but unrealistic adventurer set off for Serbia, to be joined by a motley band of volunteers, planning to liberate Bosnia-Hercegovina and Bulgaria by his own efforts and without official help from St Petersburg. More responsible nationalists in Moscow were hoping to use him to enmesh the Russian government in a war which it did not as yet want. Just as Cherniaev was arriving in Serbia in May 1876, the Tsar and Gorchakov were closely collaborating with their partners in the Three Emperors' League in an attempt to defuse the situation. The rash Serbian and Montenegrin attack, hampered rather than aided by the incompetence and insufferable behaviour of the Russian volunteers, failed disastrously. In the meantime, the Bulgarian rising of May 1876 had been crushed by the Turks with accompanying atrocities and mass murder. Although Russia managed to save Serbia by forcing the Turks to agree to an armistice in November, the sufferings of their fellow Slavs roused nationalistic feelings to such a level in St Petersburg and Moscow that Russia's unofficial foreign policy effectively seized control, with the War Minister, Miliutin, joining Ambassador Ignatiev in a call for action. The Tsar himself became convinced that war against the Turks on behalf of the Bulgarians was desirable and inevitable. Serbia and Montenegro were now seen as too independent and self-

in its expansionist aims, and rival claims to Macedonia made future war with Serbia and Greece virtually inevitable. The great powers may have established a precarious balance of power, but the Habsburgs were to prove incapable of controlling the Bosnians and Hercegovinians, with tragic consequences, and the Russians soon found their Bulgarian client to be ungrateful and unco-operative. The brutality and insensitivity of their occupying army under Prince Cherkasskii and then Dondukov alienated the Bulgarian liberals in the government, and then their nominee as prince, Alexander Battenberg. The Russians had only themselves to blame when the latter rejected the role of Russian puppet in 1883.

In a wider sense, the deep-rooted Russian resentment of Bismarck's behaviour in Berlin, and Habsburg apprehensions at Russia's expansionist behaviour effectively undermined the Three Emperors' League and paved the way for the Franco-Russian alliance of 1894. In a very real sense, the Bulgarian crisis of 1876–78 was a stepping stone on the road to the First World War.

Further Reading

Crampton, R.J. *A Short History of Modern Bulgaria* (Cambridge University Press, 1987).

Durman, K. *Lost Illusions: Russian Policies towards Bulgaria in 1877–1887* (Uppsala Studies in the Soviet Union, Almqvist and Wiksell International, 1987).

Durman, K. *The Time of the Thunderer: Mikhail Katkov, Russian Nationalist Extremism and the Failure of the Bismarckian System, 1871–1887* (East European Monographs and Columbia University Press, 1988).

Jelavich, B. *History of the Balkans, Vol. 1* (Cambridge University Press, 1983).

Kennan, F. *The Decline of Bismarck's European Order* (Princeton University Press, 1919).

MacKenzie, D. *The Serbs and Russian Panslavism, 1856–1870* (Cornell University Press, 1967).

Petrovich, M.B. *The Emergence of Russian Panslavism, 1856–1870* (Columbia University Press, 1956).

Summer, B.H. *Russia and the Balkans, 1870–1880* (Archon Books, 1962) (reprint of Oxford University Press edition of 1937).

John Morison is Senior Lecturer in Russian History at the University of Leeds.

Katharine Anne Lerman
Kaiser Wilhelm II:
Last Emperor of Imperial Germany

Imperial Germany was a very monarchical structure. Katharine Anne Lerman analyses the character of its last Emperor and his role in the years leading up to the First World War.

In 1894 a German historian called Ludwig Quidde published a pamphlet entitled 'Caligula: A Study in Roman Caesaromania'. The pamphlet purported to be about the mad Roman Emperor, Caligula. However, the spectacular success of the pamphlet, which had to be reprinted 25 times within months, and sold hundreds of thousands of copies, is attributable to the fact that it was immediately recognised to be a bold and vicious attack on the reigning German Emperor or Kaiser, Wilhelm II.

Quidde accused Kaiser Wilhelm II of 'Caesarian madness' and megalomania. More specifically, he indicted the Kaiser for his 'boundless addiction to pomp and extravagance', his flaunting of power and authority, his insatiable appetite for military triumphs, his theatricality, and his desire to conquer the oceans which bordered on a sickness. Rulers who suffered from 'caesaromania', according to Quidde, believed that they had a special relationship to God, that they had been chosen by Him and that they had a messianic mission to fulfil. Ultimately they demanded that they, too, be worshipped like a god. Altogether, in the circumstances of the 1890s, Quidde's criticism of the monarch would have amounted to a serious case of *lèse-majesté* (treason) if they had been applied directly. As it was, Quidde was lucky to escape a prolonged prison sentence.

Kaiser Wilhelm II, whom Quidde regarded as so dangerous, was only 29 years old when he became King of Prussia and German Kaiser in 1888. His reign spanned 30 momentous years during which the recently unified German Empire was transformed into an essentially modern, industrial state, embarked on an ambitious programme of naval expansion and *Weltpolitik* (world policy), and committed itself to a disastrous European war. How significant was this monarch, who has given his name to the so-called 'Wilhelmine era' in German history? Some historians have been inclined to dismiss him as a 'weak figure atop a clay pedestal' (Wehler), and an incompetent and ineffectual ruler. Contemporaries, however, asserted that there was no stronger force in Germany than the Kaiser, and that he was the supreme representative of his age.

Personality

Wilhelm II's complex and contradictory personality has long been a source of fascination and bafflement. Imperial Germany's first Chancellor, Otto von Bismarck, compared the Kaiser to a balloon which had to be held fast on a string or it would go 'no one knows whither'; the British Foreign Secretary, Sir Edward Grey, declared that Wilhelm was 'like a battleship with steam up and screws going, but with no rudder, and he will run into something some day and cause a catastrophe'. With his restless and volatile nature, the Kaiser seemed to symbolise the aggressive insecurity of a new, dynamic nation seeking a place for itself in world affairs. Moreover, as enthusiastic about modern technology, new industries and naval expansion as he was determined to uphold monarchical privilege and the traditional conservative order in Prussia, the tensions within Wilhelm's personality appeared to mirror those within 'Wilhelmine Germany' as a whole.

The Kaiser was an irascible, unpredictable man who had a strong will and took everything personally. Although, on occasion, he could be very charming, he was convinced of his divine right to rule and he refused to tolerate any kind of contradiction or systematic opposition. Indeed, he frequently asserted that he alone made German policy, that the ministers merely had to carry out his orders, and that his country 'must follow me wherever I go'. The Kaiser reserved his most savage terms of verbal abuse for the parliamentarians in the Reichstag, particularly the socialists. Among his political advisers in the 1890s it was a persistent fear that the monarch would carry out his threat to send in the army to 'shoot the lot of them' and suspend the constitution. But others, too, had to put up with his insults. 'You all know nothing,' he once told a gathering of admirals. 'Only I know something, only I decide.'

The Kaiser's personality was a matter of great concern to contemporaries who at best praised his 'splendid qualities' and 'individuality', at worst condemned his 'immaturity', 'eccentricity' and 'psychic imbalance'. Historians, too, have been preoccupied with the mental stability of a monarch who boxed Prussian ministers on the ears or whose idea of recreation was to kill 1,675 head of game on a shooting expedition at a friend's estate in December 1902 (bringing his total to date to over 50,000). Wilhelm certainly had a crude, school-boy sense of humour which could easily bring out a cruel and sadistic streak. He found it amusing to make an elderly Prussian general pretend he was a dog and jump over a stick; and one of the most notorious incidents in his reign occurred at the height of the *Daily Telegraph* affair in November 1908 when the Chief of his Military Cabinet, who was 56 years old and over six feet tall, dressed up as a ballerina and danced for him. It was not the first time that General Dietrich von Hülsen-Haeseler had performed in this way to amuse and distract the Kaiser, but the deep depression into which Wilhelm had sunk at the onset of the domestic crisis was certainly not alleviated when, while dancing, his adviser died of a heart attack.

Early life

The complexities of the Kaiser's personality have encouraged historians to comb his early life for psychological insights. Wilhelm was the eldest child of Crown Prince Friedrich of Prussia (later briefly Kaiser Friedrich III) and his wife, Victoria, the daughter of Queen Victoria; and without doubt Wilhelm's ambivalent attitude to the British and his recurring anglophobia can be traced in no small part to the difficult relationship he had with his mother, who was the dominant partner in the Anglo-German marriage. During his adolescence Wilhelm become estranged from his parents both personally and politically, and when his father died in 1888 he even had the royal palace surrounded by troops to prevent his mother removing any secret papers to England. But all his life Wilhelm had difficulty trying to reconcile his English and German identities for, although thoroughly inculcated with Prussian values, he grew up in a very English household. As German Kaiser he felt himself to be essentially English. His only regular daily newspaper was the English *Daily Graphic*.

Wilhelm's mother complained about his hyperactivity as a child, and a number of those who came into close contact with the Kaiser as an adult, including his best friend, Philipp zu Eulenburg, questioned whether he was completely sane or normal. Recent historical assessments have suggested that he was a narcissistically disturbed personality, and that he may have suffered from a congenital brain disorder which was aggravated by a lack of oxygen during his birth. The circumstances of Wilhelm's birth on 27 January 1859 are well documented; after an exhausting labour in which the Crown Princess was given a considerable quantity of chloroform, the royal prince initially appeared lifeless. In addition, Wilhelm was to suffer a permanent physical disability. Since the baby was in breech position with its arms over its head, the obstetrician had to pull its left arm forcibly down to its side before it could be delivered. As a result Wilhelm's left arm never developed properly and always remained several inches shorter than his right. Not only were his left arm and hand virtually paralysed, but the whole of the left side of his body was affected. The young prince had difficulty keeping his balance and developed an awkward posture. As an adult he needed help in dressing and cutting up his food.

While most observers admired the way in which Wilhelm II came to terms with his physical disability, it is clear that it must have had psychological consequences. There is extensive evidence that Wilhelm never succeeded in living up to the high expectations of his anxious and disappointed mother. Moreover, from babyhood the young Prussian prince had to undergo a series of often bizarre treatments for his arm, which included saltwater or malt baths, low levels of electric current and 'animal baths' when the left arm – which was very cold – was warmed for half an hour inside the body of a freshly killed hare. Wilhelm had his right arm strapped to his body for a period every day to encourage him to use his left one. Learning to ride was also a distressing and humiliating ordeal, but one which he accomplished successfully under the supervision of his strict and humourless Calvinist tutor, Hinzpeter.

Power and privileges

Wilhelm II's personality and upbringing would not hold such fascination for historians were it not for the fact that he occupied what Eulenburg described as 'the most powerful throne in the world'. The German Empire, founded in 1871, was the most dynamic state in Europe in the decades before 1914, with a rapidly growing population and expanding industrial economy. Moreover, its political system was not parliamentary or democratic, but left executive power in the hands of a small ruling élite which was appointed directly by the monarch. Thus the German Kaiser was no mere figurehead but wielded enormous political power. As King of Prussia, the largest German federal state, he enjoyed virtually autocratic powers which were only limited by the emasculated constitution of 1851, a remnant of the revolutionary upheavals of 1848. As German Kaiser, Wilhelm was sovereign in matters of foreign policy, having the right to declare war and conclude peace. He also enjoyed personal command over the army and navy, controlled all personnel appointments in the Reich (imperial) administration, and had the right to dissolve the Reichstag.

It was the Kaiser's right to appoint and dismiss all ministers and officials in the Prussian and Reich executives which proved to be his crucial prerogative in the constitutional struggles of the 1890s. Wilhelm II aspired to rule personally and in 1890 he dismissed the 'Iron Chancellor', Bismarck. During the protracted political crisis which followed, the implications of the imperial German constitution gradually became apparent. Not one of Bismarck's successors as Chancellor was able to match his power, prestige and authority. The Kaiser, aided by Eulenburg and other 'irresponsible' friends, was able to thwart the evolution of a more collective form of government, dismissing ministers who opposed his will and install-ing in their place new men who recognised that they owed their positions and allegiance exclusively to him. By 1897 even the Chancellor, Chlodwig zu Hohenlohe-Schillingsfürst, had capitu-lated to the will of the Crown and accepted what was essentially a subordinate role. In 1900, when Eulenburg's close friend, Bernhard von Bülow, became Chancellor, the pivot of government effectively became the confidential relationship between Chancellor and Kaiser. Beneath them the Prussian ministers and Reich state secre-taries were submissive, pliant and, above all, isolated.

The 'Personal rule' debate

Bülow had anticipated this system of government in the 1890s as 'personal rule – in the good sense', and he believed that it was the only way that the German Empire which Bismarck had created could survive the rule of Kaiser Wilhelm II without a major upheaval. Throughout his reign the Kaiser was attacked by contem-porary critics for practising 'personal rule'. The attacks reached their height during the *Daily Telegraph* affair of 1908 when Wilhelm's indiscretions to the British newspaper prompted a public clamour for constitutional guarantees and limitations to the monarch's power.

Nevertheless, many modern historians have been understandably reluctant to accept the thesis that the Kaiser personally ruled Germany before 1914. Not only does this thesis seem perilously close to the 'great man' theory of history, but it also appears to underestimate the complexity of the imperial German political system, the influence of the other states and political institutions within the Empire, and the inevitable constraints on the exercise of monarchical authority. Moreover, on close examination of policy issues, it is quite clear that the Kaiser did not rule Germany on a day to day basis or have command of the details of government work. His knowledge and understanding of political matters was always very superficial and dilettantist; he disliked routine work and read newspaper cuttings in preference to political reports; and his life was an endless whirl of state occasions, social events, military manoeuvres, court ceremonies, parades, cruises and hunt-ing trips, most of which involved the restless and peripatetic Kaiser in prolonged absences from Berlin. The one major issue in which Wilhelm II's will is generally seen to have been decisive is in the building of a German navy. The Kaiser was determined to have 'his ships', whether cruisers or battleships, and he consistently supported all proposals for naval expansion from 1888.

A preoccupation with the Kaiser's political initiatives and actions tends to encourage the conclusion that his 'personal rule' was a myth, and that the monarch merely interfered with or meddled in political decision-making, thereby contributing to, but in no sense determining the erratic course of German policy before 1914. Indeed, the overall impression of Wilhelmine government is one of a fundamental failure to co-ordinate government policy at the highest level and a considerable degree of confusion in decision-making, both of which can be taken to signify Wilhelm II's deficiencies and inadequacies as a leader rather than his strong personal role.

The Kaiser's regime

Such a conclusion, however, completely underestimates the significance of the Kaiser and obscures the nature of the political system over which he presided. It ignores the extent to which Wilhelm II's personality impressed itself on the German executive and, in particular, how the latter crucially was and remained *his* government. Since the Kaiser appointed and dismissed all members of the Reich and Prussian executives, he determined the parameters of what was and was not possible in terms of policy. There was no possibility that any major decisions could be taken without his concurrence. As one state secretary of the Reich Colonial Office later admitted, 'given the nature of the ruler, it was completely irrelevant who was minister at any one time'. All the ministers were equally powerless, without support in the parliaments or among the people, and dependent on 'managing' the Kaiser if there was to be any semblance of government. They had no means of opposing the monarch if they were determined to keep their privileges, and in the last analysis were confronted with a clear choice between obedience and dismissal.

The Kaiser had a controlling and corrupting influence over personnel appointments, and the effects of his patronage reverberated throughout the entire bureaucracy. Prussian ministers, state secretaries and officials found that their power and influence waxed and waned in accordance with the favour and goodwill bestowed on them by the monarch. Wilhelm, for his part, selected men for personal rather than political reasons, surrounding himself with royal favourites who were not infrequently inadequate to their tasks. Between 1897 and 1900 Bülow, as state secretary of the Foreign Office, exerted more authority within the executive than his formal superior, the Chancellor, Hohenlohe, because he was known to be the Kaiser's favourite. As Chancellor, Bülow organised his day around the cultivation of his close relationship with Wilhelm, and was prepared to devote several hours to the task.

The military monarchy

Moreover, the Kaiser was not merely of central importance in the civilian government of Wilhelmine Germany, but he also stood at the pinnacle of the quite separate military hierarchy. Constitutionally there was no scope for any interference in the Kaiser's 'power of command' and effective political control could only be exerted over the army through the Kaiser. However incompetent Wilhelm II was as 'supreme war lord' and co-ordinator of the armed forces, the army remained the monarch's personal weapon, owing its loyalty and obedience exclusively to him.

The potential political significance of this relationship between the Kaiser and the army can scarcely be exaggerated. Wilhelm II surrounded himself with military men and invariably appeared in military uniform. He often chose generals in preference to bureaucrats for positions of state, and, unlike ministers, generals had the right of direct access to the monarch whenever they wished. In the early years of Wilhelm's reign the German Foreign Office fretted that his military and naval attachés were running a kind of parallel diplomatic service, circumventing the official diplomatic channels. After 1908, when Wilhelm's closest civilian friends, Philipp zu Eulenburg and the so-called 'Liebenberg circle', had to be banned from court in the wake of allegations concerning their homosexuality, the influence of his military entourage was unrivalled.

Repeatedly, when it came to a clash between military and civilian authority, Wilhelm took the army's side. In 1913 his willingness to defend army transgressions in Zabern, a town in Alsace, precipitated a political crisis and revealed the extent to which Wilhelmine Germany was a military monarchy rather than a constitutional state. The growing influence of the army in the years immediately before 1914 can also be seen to have had fateful consequences with respect to the origins of the First World War. The idea of a victorious, 'preventative war' as a solution to the monarchy's problems had some of its most ardent supporters within Wilhelm II's military entourage.

The role of Kaiser Wilhelm II

In Wilhelmine Germany the hereditary monarch thus still possessed political, military and social power. All chains of political and

imperialism in ways which suggested that its development marked a terminal phase in the evolution of capitalism.

Such attempts at precision, however, have been increasingly overshadowed by the widespread association of imperialism with political propaganda and partisan abuse. Beginning, perhaps, with the passionate conflicts generated by the South African War (1899–1902), and fuelled by the rivalries of the Cold War after 1945, imperialism has become a commonplace and lost much of its systematic content.

If it is hard to say that imperialism has any commonly agreed content, it is of course possible to attempt one's own definition. The following is just one, which highlights the idea of imperialism as a process:

> the extension of formal controls by a powerful state over one or a number of other weaker peoples or states, often of a different race or culture.

However, even such an anodyne definition raises all kinds of difficulties, and perhaps two in particular.

Where, for instance, does imperialism begin and end? Do we have to think simply of the links between European and non-European areas? What about the possibility of imperialism inside Europe? In recent years historians like Michael Hechter have developed the idea of 'internal colonialism' to refer to the common phenomenon of weaker, less-developed areas dominated by or tributary to stronger, more prosperous centres. This can be seen in the relationship of regions within single states, for example in that of the Massif Central and Brittany to other parts of France, in the links between northern and southern Italy, or those of Wales and south-west England to the London-centred south-east. It may exist in the developing links between countries – in the processes by which German influence expanded into south-east Europe, and Portugal emerged on Europe's periphery, subject to all the restraints imposed by substantial financial dependence on France and Germany.

This reference to Portugal raises questions about the type of control associated with imperialism. Does it have to involve formal political rule? While it may appear to simplify matters to say 'yes', historians have been dissatisfied with the simple equation of imperialism and the imposition of direct political control. They are conscious that substantial influence or degrees of control over states have existed without the need for annexation or direct rule. This can result, for example, from the expansion of trade, emigration and investment to the point where the influence and activities of

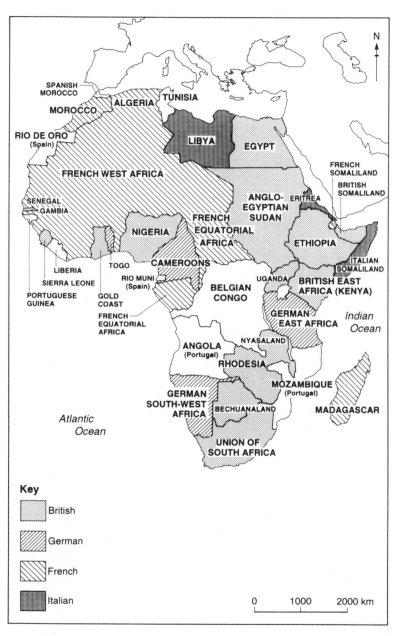

Africa after Partition, 1914

foreigners could be of decisive political, social and economic import-ance, especially if backed even by limited force. The nineteenth-century consequences, for example, of expanding French trade and investment in North Africa (especially Egypt), and of Britain's growing interests in Argentina, have led to important distinctions between 'formal' and 'informal' empire and to prolonged debate about the so-called 'imperialism of free trade'.

The expansion of Europe

The overt signs both of Europe's imperial expansion in the later nineteenth century and of its various degrees of formality are, of course, inescapable. In South-East Asia during the period from the late 1850s to the early 1890s Laos, Cambodia, Annam and Tonkin were conquered by the French, and the Dutch extended their control in Java, Borneo, and Sumatra. In China substantial Euro-pean footholds were acquired in 1842 and 1858–60 after the Opium Wars; between 1885 and 1900 spheres of influence were claimed in southern China by Britain and France, Germany took Shantung, and the Italians leased Ningpo. The Russian presence established in northern China represented only the final stage of her restless expansion into central and east Asia. The Pacific was similarly carved up into spheres, with the French and British in Polynesia, the Germans in Samoa and New Guinea, while locally Australians and New Zealanders developed comparable territorial ambitions. Most dramatically the Europeans partitioned Africa, extending their claims and presence beyond the limited footholds held in 1870, until in 1900, only Liberia and Abyssinia remained independent. Portugal reasserted claims based on her historic presence in Angola and Mozambique; Belgians acquired the Congo; the British expanded in southern Africa, the Gold Coast, Nigeria, Kenya and Uganda, Egypt and the Sudan; France took the Western Sudan, Madagascar, and parts of both north and west Africa; other areas fell to Italy, Germany and Spain. Imperial expansion, moreover, was not con-fined to European powers: Japan pushed forward into Korea and on to the Chinese mainland at Amoy, while the United States took over Spanish possessions in the Caribbean and the Philippines.

This global transformation in the late nineteenth century has naturally both excited great curiosity and stimulated many attempts at explanation. Among the most persistent or long-lived accounts of the process are those which have emphasised the political or diplomatic roots of imperialism: essentially it represented the trans-fer overseas of Europe's diplomatic rivalries. European govern-ments developing nationalistic ambitions, while constrained after 1870 by the crystallisation of a new balance of power and their fears of another continental war, switched their attention to extra-European problems and competition.

Differing interpretations

This approach owed much to the early study of Bismarck's diplomacy, and was enshrined in influential works such as A.J.P. Taylor's *Germany's First Bid for Colonies* (1938). Historians stressed the impetus given to imperial rivalries by Germany's persistent concern to keep Britain and France at odds. They noted especially Bismarck's exploitation of Britain's difficulties in Egypt in order to win French gratitude; they interpreted his colonial initiatives of 1884–85 as designed to illustrate for Britain her need for good relations with Germany and the danger of isolation. Thereafter German policies in the Mediterranean, the Turkish Empire, and South Africa were dictated, it was argued, by the wish to push Britain closer to the Triple Alliance. In the same way, Britain's encouragement of Italian ambitions in Tripoli and Somalia and her concessions to French interests in parts of west Africa were seen as reflections of her need to maintain the continental balance.

Closely allied to such calculations and providing further essentially 'political' explanations of imperialism are suggestions that European powers were thereby seeking to impress both themselves and others by demonstrating their self-confidence, strength and practical capability. In particular, the French scholar Henry Brunschwig has made much of this 'imperialism of prestige'. He has argued that French interest in expansion was fuelled by the national need to efface the disgrace and losses of the Franco-Prussian War. Such a general preoccupation can be linked to the deterioration in Anglo-French relations in Africa during the 1870s, and to French jealousy of British activity in Egypt in the 1880s. Britain's invasion of Egypt in 1882 not only upstaged the French but did so in a region traditionally considered one of French predominance. Similarly, the desire to redeem martial reputations and re-establish military careers has been detected in the continuing prominence of France's local forces in pushing forward French imperial frontiers as distant from each other as those in the Sudan and Indochina. Italy, as a newly-established state, saw in the acquisition of colonies testimony to her arrival on the world's stage; Germans were perhaps too ready to see in their own lack of imperial possessions evidence that others wished to restrict them to an inferior position. In the case of Portugal, such was the sentimental importance attached to historic possessions that its monarchs supported the defence and expansion of its colonies to win popularity and ward off republicanism (unsuccessfully, as the events of 1910 were to prove).

In a world where it was widely held that the great powers of the future were likely to be large empires, suggestions that existing nation states should try as far as possible to match in size the United States or Russia had a certain plausibility. In Germany the *Kolonialverein* (Colonial Union) and the *Gesellschaft für deutsche Kolonisation* (German Colonisation Company), formed in the early 1880s, were both popular and aimed to promote colonial growth and overseas settlements as the hallmarks of national greatness. It likewise seemed natural to many contemporaries that Britain, with her head start, should pursue a dual policy, consolidating both politically and defensively her existing colonies and developing imperial economic resources, especially in her latest tropical acquisitions. In these ways the enthusiasms of the Imperial Federation League, founded in 1884, were taken up and extended by Joseph Chamberlain and his supporters after 1895.

Notions of prestige, national self-esteem and international standing undoubtedly joined hands in the last quarter of the century with hardening racial attitudes. To the long-standing belief in Europe as the highest source of civilised values, expressed either in western secular knowledge or the Christian religion, was added the heightened sense of superiority over non-Europeans which resulted from continued technological progress, the accumulated experience of colonial rule, and evolutionary thought. In varying degrees, therefore, different European nationals developed the idea of their own country's particular civilising mission; widespread confidence in the inevitability or the benefits of expanded European control made it easier to ignore local resistance and to override indigenous rights, especially if other interests strengthened the case for intervention. Thus, German statesmen had no compunction in using the murder of a missionary in November 1897 as the pretext for seizing the Chinese port of Kiaowchow. Such high-handed reactions and grossly disproportionate responses by Europeans to local incidents and protests were not uncommon. The French pursuit of Samory in West Africa, the British handling of Jaja or of the Asante and Zulu kingdoms, the German war against the Herero in South-West Africa, and the combined European response to China's Boxer rebellion are only some of the most striking examples.

Social imperialism

In recent years interpretations such as these, which attempt to root imperialism above all in metropolitan diplomacy or general intellectual outlooks, have come under vigorous attack from historians convinced that social and economic circumstances deserve to be given much greater weight. Of particular importance is the now fashionable concept of 'social imperialism'. This embodies the idea that politicians facing social conflict and serious political challenge at home have often played the imperial card as a way out of their difficulties. They have done so in part, perhaps, simply to provide a diversion from domestic troubles. But they have also had the defensive political aim of rallying conservative forces, as well as hopes that empire might provide the material basis for greater prosperity and a measure of social reform.

Here again Germany's history provided the initial key. The concept was developed by H.U. Wehler in order to explain Bismarck's sudden colonial initiatives in South-West Africa and Tanganyika and the subsequent development after 1895 of Germany's 'Weltpolitik'. Wehler assumed the central importance of domestic policy for any effective explanation of imperialism. He argued that after 1870 Germany was not only undergoing rapid and unstable industrialisation but was also facing a mounting agrarian crisis. Bismarck's turn to protectionism, his adoption of social welfare reforms, and his responses to imperialist pressure groups were fundamentally related to aspects of a single policy designed to curb social tensions and nullify forceful political challenges from the left. Later colonial and naval policies were similarly inspired.

For some time this approach seemed to have little applicability outside Germany, but since 1975 historians of Britain, France and Italy have argued for its wider relevance. Joseph Chamberlain has long attracted the label of 'social imperialist', but in recent articles Freda Harcourt has also extended it to Disraeli and Gladstone. Studies by American historians have argued that the imperial policies of the Third Republic hinged on ministerial preoccupation with domestic stability. In each case, overseas expansion has been presented as having its place in varying measure alongside protective tariffs and social welfare legislation in a carefully calculated programme of political management intended to still the class conflicts of Europe's advanced industrial societies.

It should not be thought that 'social imperialism' has gone unchallenged. Wehler's 'social imperialist' Bismarck has won little support, and the concept is now clearly felt to obscure the true relations between economy, society and politics in the years before 1914. Applied to France, it has again been dismissed as almost certainly too crude to do justice either to the country's regional diversity or to the period's political complexity. Chamberlain's failures may perhaps be taken as one indicator of the limited relevance of 'social imperialism' to Britain's experience. Nevertheless a vigorous debate continues, providing a constant reminder that the impulses contributing to imperial expansion are to be looked for in many areas of national life.

The economic interpretation

Social imperialist policies, however conceived, are of course very closely related to the economic circumstances of late nineteenth-century Europe, notably to the conditions of 'the Great Depression' after 1873. The idea that imperialism was somehow connected to the economic uncertainty of the period is an old one, shared by active participants and contemporary theorists alike. Historians have therefore had little difficulty in picking out general characteristics of the period's economic life which helped to encourage imperial ambitions on the part of private entrepreneurs and sometimes of governments.

There was a marked growth of industrial rivalry, as Germany and the United States in particular challenged Britain's hitherto leading position. This was associated with both falling prices and mounting protectionism after 1875, notably in Germany (1879, 1890, 1902), France (1871–2, 1881, 1892) and the USA (1890, 1897). The growth of industrial production contributed to the rising concern for secure raw material supplies, both old, like gold or iron ore, and new, like rubber and copper for the new electrical industries. Worries about adequate markets also abounded: quite apart from the need to absorb rising levels of production, if traditional foreign markets were obstructed or even closed by protective tariff policies, new ones would be required.

A general economic context taken by itself, however, is not enough. Historians must go on to ask some very specific questions. For example, is it possible to find individuals or pressure groups with these interests and worries pressing for imperial expansion? Undoubtedly the answer to this is 'yes'. In the early phases of the 'Great Depression' there was widespread European interest in Central Africa, in expectation of its commercial potential; others sceptical of this potential nevertheless saw substantial opportunities for gain simply from the process of opening up the African continent, building railways, and obtaining mineral or land claims. Belgian, Dutch and French as well as British concessionaires constantly badgered European and non-European authorities to make over monopoly rights for a pittance. In West Africa, for example, pre-emptive annexations were called for by chambers of commerce everywhere, as fears grew that foreign action might restrict mercantile ambitions. In particular British and German free-traders dreaded Portuguese or French intervention with its threat of exclusive tariffs. Access to the Niger river, and even more in Asia to the Mekong or Yangtse with their openings to the immeasurable China market, became matters of intense concern. Leopold II was able to exploit such fears and so persuade European powers, anxious to keep the

Congo basin open for their own traders, to recognise his oversight of the vastly extensive Congo Free State in 1885.

Problems in the analysis of imperialism, however, do not end with establishing the existence of economic ambitions. Historians have to do more: in particular, they must try to explain and demonstrate how such demands or pressures were linked to the actual decisions of governments to intervene or annex. No other governments demonstrated an enthusiasm for empire comparable to Leopold's, but they may have felt it at least politically expedient to pander to the demands of particular lobbies, both in Africa and elsewhere, even if they did not entirely share their concerns or had quite different priorities. Such shifting relationships are rarely easy to chart or demonstrate. In any assessment of official actions, for example, it is important never to forget the relative insignificance to metropolitan countries in direct economic terms of those areas caught up in the wave of imperial expansion between 1860 and 1914. This is clearly the case whether one looks, for instance, at the direction of European trade, at the relative importance to individual countries of different areas of the globe, or at the direction and volume of overseas investment.

The economics of empire

The empire-builders of the late nineteenth century were increasingly trading with each other and with advanced industrialising economies, rather than with tropical or undeveloped countries and colonial territories. By far the greater proportion of Britain's trade continued to be with Europe and North America – 65.9% in 1860, 63.3% in 1913. India continued to be her most important colonial trading partner, Canada and Argentina were the regions of most rapid increase in her trade and foreign investment; yet none of them were areas significantly involved in the late-century burst of empire-building. New French investment abroad between 1892 and 1914 totalled 35.2bn francs, of which 38% went to Russia and the Balkans, 21% to the Americas, and at most only 11% to her own colonies. Of Germany's exports, the share taken by her colonies only grew from 0.17% to 0.73% between 1891 and 1910, and the proportion sent to Asia as a whole was never more than 7.5%.

While such figures help to put the nineteenth century's formal imperialism into perspective, it has been argued that there are more helpful ways of analysing the economic dynamics and importance of imperial expansion. There is, first, the suggestion that many territories were acquired simply as an insurance policy; while they might be of marginal current value, they were felt to be of real potential significance for the future, and, even if expensive for the time being, were useful in boosting present confidence. Whether or not their advantages were eventually realised, and in what manner this was done, are not questions which can be answered over any short period of time. There are also arguments which accept the economic insignificance of colonies in macro-economic terms, but emphasise their great importance at a lower level to certain sectors, regional interests or individual firms. This has been underlined, for example, by studies of French imperialism. These point to the value of certain possessions to the textile producers of Alsace, the industrialists of Lyons, the importers of minerals from North Africa, and the commercial interests in Marseilles and Bordeaux. While most bankers and investors were little interested in colonial opportunities, there can be found others – in the *Banque de l'Indochine*, or the *Banque de Paris et des Pays Bas* – who were. Comparable examples can be found in both Britain and Portugal. Finally, some historians argue that imperialism must be understood as a world-wide economic system, manifested in both formal and informal ways, serving in different times and places industrial, commercial and financial interests. Individual nation states in their role as imperialist powers are therefore best studied in terms of the global range of their economic activities, and particular attention should be given to the changing contribution made by the latter to their balance of payments.

All three approaches are hotly debated. They not only bring us back again to the problem of distinguishing between formal and informal empire, but raise fundamental questions about the relationship between 'political' and 'economic' factors in explaining imperialism. It is essential to distinguish where possible between the pressures of particular importance which encouraged the extension of imperial influence and control, the purposes to which territorial acquisitions were put, and the interests served by different forms of economic expansion abroad. Without such analytical distinctions 'imperialism' is likely to remain an unhelpful term if not an incomprehensible phenomenon.

The role of the periphery

Finally, it is important to recognise that European imperialism cannot be understood if one looks only at Europe itself, at its economy, its states system, and the ideas or prejudices of its peoples. The nature and timing of imperial expansion were also crucially affected by events on what historians have come to call, for want of a better word, 'the periphery'. This can be illustrated in general terms by referring again to the economic circumstances of the period. The effects of the late nineteenth-century depression were felt not only by Europeans but by their trading partners abroad. The fall in prices of manufactured goods was more than matched by that of many raw materials and foodstuffs. As a result, non-European suppliers and merchants anxious to halt the decline in their incomes, and non-European governments concerned about their commercial revenues, attempted to tighten their control over the conditions of trade. Depression thus bred much fiercer competition, illegality and violence both amongst Europeans themselves and between Europeans and non-Europeans. This process of mounting conflict brought increasing pressure first on local European officials and then on metropolitan governments to intervene in defence of their nationals' interests. Intervention by one European state, or its probability, encouraged moves by others.

This pattern of intervention was not new, but undoubtedly became much more widespread from the late 1870s. The way in which it gathered momentum has been especially well portrayed in the case of West Africa, notably by scholars such as J.D. Hargreaves, A.G. Hopkins and C.W. Newbury, and D.K. Fieldhouse has extended the analysis on a global scale. This is no place to rehearse the details of their work. It is more important to recognise that in developing their ideas, these historians were in effect building on an insight originally expounded by Ronald Robinson and John Gallagher in their book *Africa and the Victorians* (1961; 2nd edn., 1981). Rejecting older views of a 'new' imperialism after 1870 generated within Europe and simply imposed on the outside world, Robinson and Gallagher emphasised instead how the gradual process of Europe's expansion – economic, military, religious, and by migration or settlement overseas – both undermined the stability of non-European societies and provoked 'nationalist' resistance to the European presence. The development of an unstable 'periphery' was thus an essential precursor of formal imperial expansion, especially in areas where instability seemed to threaten important European interests.

Focusing on the examples of Egypt and South Africa, Robinson and Gallagher argued that local resistance threatened Britain's strategic control of the vital routes to India. Successive British governments staggered reluctantly along the paths to occupation and annexation as the only means, it seemed, to restore a stable political framework within which those strategic interests could be protected. Together with the further argument that the partition of Africa as a whole was fuelled at critical points by Egyptian and South African crises, their thesis has always been regarded as brilliantly developed but nevertheless controversial. Just now it is meeting a renewed challenge, from historians who believe that its inattention to economic issues necessitates a return to the examination of Europe's metropolitan economies.

Whatever the outcome of this exciting debate, however, it is no longer possible to ignore the importance of events remote from Europe itself when seeking to understand Europe's imperialism. In many ways it is most unhelpful to think of 'imperialism' as simply propelled from Europe. The 'European imperialism' referred to in my title may in fact be something of a misnomer for development so dependent for their pattern on the interaction of the European and non-European worlds.[1]

Note

(1) For a further discussion of these ideas, see Porter, A.N. *European Imperialism 1860–1914* (Macmillan, 1994).

Andrew N. Porter is Rhodes Professor of Imperial History at King's College, London. He is the author of many articles and books including *The Origins of the South African War* (Manchester University Press, 1980) and, with Stockwell, A.J. *British Imperial Policy and Decolonisation 1938–1964* (2 vols., Macmillan, 1987, 1989). He has recently edited *An Atlas of British Overseas Expansion* (Routledge, 1991, 1994).

John C.G. Röhl
Imperial Germany: The Riddle of 1914

John C.G. Röhl reconsiders an event and controversy which has scarred Germany's psyche and historiography for most of the twentieth century. He explores the causes of the First World War and the historiographical controversies that have raged ever since. In the process he delivers some warnings about the use and misuse of historical evidence in the national interest and examines the evidence that Wilhelmine Germany desired and planned a general war.

Ever since the First World War began, in 1914, historians have been locked in controversy about its causes. Indeed, considering the length and violence of the debate, its global scope and the fundamental issues it raises, many would regard the War Guilt Controversy, as it used to be known, as the historical controversy *par excellence*. In this brief survey I wish to look at some of the key moments in that debate, and to convey some idea of why, with so many historians of so many nationalities poring over the documentary record for so long, the issue was not resolved long ago, and why it is still so contentious today.

Introduction

I shall start by looking in rather broad terms at the first phase of the debate, from 1914 to about 1960. But first a few preliminary observations. I shall be talking about the causes of the First World War largely at the decision-making level, but I want to make it very clear that I have absolutely no wish to deny that there were deeper causes at work as well. The different growth rates of the populations of the various countries of Europe, the varying performance and needs of their economies, mass participation in nationalist and socialist movements, the influence of the press and of intellectuals on mass politics and government thinking, the presence or absence of a sense of domestic crisis, the ability or otherwise of governments to tap national economic resources and popular enthusiasm to build up military machines, the burden, in turn, which the military machine in each country imposed on economic growth, the rivalry of those military machines with one another internationally, the extent to which civilian statesmen were able to control the military men, the geographical location and hence strategic dilemma of each

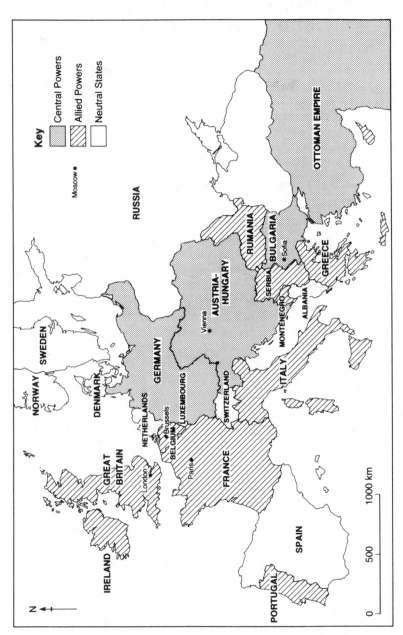

Europe into the First World War

Key

- Central Powers
- Allied Powers
- Neutral States

NORWAY

SWEDEN

DENMARK

RUSSIA

Moscow

GREAT BRITAIN

London

IRELAND

NETHERLANDS

Brussels

BELGIUM

LUXEMBOURG

GERMANY

Vienna

AUSTRIA-HUNGARY

FRANCE

SWITZERLAND

ITALY

MONTENEGRO

SERBIA

RUMANIA

BULGARIA

Sofia

ALBANIA

GREECE

OTTOMAN EMPIRE

Paris

PORTUGAL

SPAIN

N

0   500   1000 km

major Power, the historical accident of whether they had engaged in the imperialist scramble in good time or arrived on the scene too late for the choicest pickings – all these are obviously factors of vital importance that have to be borne in mind in any discussion of the causes of war in 1914, just as the ententes and alliances and military conventions signed by the Great Powers in the decades before the war had an obvious but crucial bearing on the thinking and policies of the statesmen of each of those countries when the crisis came in that fateful summer.

Moreover, the consequences of the war were hardly any less profound than these deeper social, economic, ideological, military and diplomatic causes. Historians have rightly described the First World War as the 'basic catastrophe' – the *Urkatastrophe* – of our century, as the catastrophe out of which so many others were born. Out of the First World War grew fascism in Italy and national socialism in Germany, though in both cases of course there were deeper roots as well; and out of national socialism came the Second World War with all its human horrors and terrible political consequences. The First World War ended in the collapse of the German, Austrian, Russian and Turkish Empires, and thus led to the setting up of new but unstable small states from the Baltic to the Adriatic and Black Sea and beyond. The 1914–18 war also marked the beginning of the end of the British and French overseas empires, the coming to power of the Bolsheviks in Russia, and the first military involvement of the young United States of America in the Old World. It is not exaggeration, therefore, to see in the Great War the cauldron in which were forged many of the distinguished features of the world in which we now live. We should consequently not be surprised to find that the issue of how and why that war began still touches on many a raw nerve and that the debate continues to arouse very deep passions.

However, to argue that an event had deep causes and profound consequences is surely not to say that the deep causes were *sufficient* in themselves to bring about the event. It is my belief that the deeper causes to which I have referred were *necessary*, certainly, to produce the kind of war which broke out in 1914, but that those deeper factors (which had after all been present in the European situation for several decades prior to the outbreak of war) did not lead *by themselves* to a self-activation of war. The deeper causes, then, were *necessary* but not *sufficient*. What is still missing is the decision-making dimension: the decisions and indecisions, the intentions and illusions and errors of the few men who in each country held that mysterious thing called power.

The 'war guilt' controversy 1914–1960

As soon as war broke out, each side publicly accused the other of unprovoked aggression, whilst protesting its own innocence. Interestingly, however, during the war itself German and Austrian political and military leaders were ready to admit *in private* that the decision to begin war had actually been taken in Berlin and Vienna. We now possess a large number of sources to this effect, most notably the recently published war time diaries of the Berlin newspaper editor Theodor Wolff. In countless conversations with the 'men of 1914' – Bethmann, Jagow, Stumm, Lichnowsky and many others – Wolff gained clear and unequivocal admissions that the Berlin leaders had actually wanted (*gewollt*) war in 1914, in expectation of a quick victory over France and Russia, and in the belief that, since war appeared inevitable, it was militarily better for Germany to start it now than to fight in less favourable circumstances two or three years later. Recent research by British and American historians has also revealed a desperately strong desire for war present in the very highest military and diplomatic circles in Vienna. The Austro-Hungarian Chief of Staff General Franz Freiherr Conrad von Hötzendorff was virtually screaming for war for several years before Sarajevo, and after the assassination an influential group of 'young Aehrenthalians' in the Vienna Foreign Office, among them Count Hoyos, were equally persuaded that the Habsburg Monarchy could only be saved from disintegration by war. No such admissions have come to light in England, France and Russia, and indeed, in logic they could not exist, unless one posits that both sides secretly conspired to begin war simultaneously.

Of course, as soon as the war was lost, the German side could not admit, for compelling political reasons, that it bore the major responsibility for the outbreak of war in 1914. German statesmen and scholars now retreated to a position where all the belligerent Powers were said to have been equally responsible, i.e. no one Power or group of Powers was responsible, i.e. impersonal forces – the system, not men; deeper factors, not decisions – had caused war. At times the causes given were so deep, so general, so abstract that this seemed to have been a war without a cause.

This line was maintained throughout the 1920s and 1930s with such vigour – and with substantial assistance, financial as well as moral, from the German Foreign Office – that long before the Second World War broke out, the 'Anglo-Saxon' view had begun to crumble – and with it the Treaty of Versailles, which had been predicated on the 'war guilt of Germany and her allies'. Of crucial importance in this inter-war period was the work of two American historians, Barnes and Fay, who incidentally were in close touch with the ex-Kaiser and other leaders of Imperial Germany, and who were hoodwinked into endorsing the German position. It is interesting to ask why British and French historians were unable at that time to mount a convincing counter-argument. Their inability to read German well, their unfamiliarity with the old Gothic handwriting, were clearly important factors – but most important of all was a German conspiracy to withhold from them the archival records that mattered. German archivists even withheld sensitive documents from German scholars (such as George Hallgarten and Eckart Kehr) whom they classified as untrustworthy and unpatriotic.

After 1945 this German tradition at first continued without a break. Only a handful of German history professors were banned from teaching by the Allies; the remainder stayed at their posts, continuing to maintain in public a line which some of them at any rate knew to be untrue. In fact, to insist on Germany's 'innocence' in 1914 had become politically more compelling than ever for them since the 'German catastrophe' of 1933–45. Though the Treaty of Versailles was now dead and buried, the loss of vast eastern territories to Poland and Russia, the abolition by Allied decree of the State of Prussia and the division of the remainder of Germany into two mutually hostile states, meant that even more was at stake than had been in the inter-war years. If Germany were shown to have been the aggressor in 1914 as well as in 1939, the entire shape of German history would alter. In the late 1940s and throughout the 1950s, German historians were arguing that the Prussian military tradition had culminated not in Nazism but in the unsuccessful 20 July 1944 attempt of German officers to assassinate the 'tyrant' and 'demagogue' Hitler. If Germany were now to be blamed for starting war in 1914 as well as 1939, those 'patriotic' and 'conservative' Prussian and Imperial values would be discredited as having led to two World Wars and as having paved the way for Hitler's Third Reich. A reunification of the two Germanies and the re-acquisition of the eastern lands would then be void of all moral and political legitimation. As one leading archivist put it in 1962: 'with a new war guilt thesis we would lose the Cold Third World War as well!'

The Fischer controversy

This archivist was of course referring to Fritz Fischer's famous book *Griff nach der Weltmacht* which had been published in the previous year. Fischer was the first German university professor to step out of line and openly support the 'Anglo-Saxon' interpretation of German history, much to the surprise of Anglo-Saxon historians who had abandoned that position in the 1920s. Fischer's intervention was so telling because it was based on a huge mountain of documentary evidence detailing the extent of German war aims throughout the First World War. The key document in the book was a position paper written by the German Chancellor Theobald von Bethmann Hollweg on 9 September 1914 stating that the 'general aim of the war' was the 'security of the German Reich in west and east for all imaginable time', and asserting that 'for this purpose France must be so weakened as to make her revival as a great power impossible for all time. Russia must be thrust back as far as possible from Germany's eastern frontier and her domination of the non-Russian vassal peoples broken'. Bethmann's 'September Programme' then went on to spell out in detail how this general aim was to be achieved in practice: parts of France were to be annexed, France was to pay a war indemnity so large that it would be impossible for her to afford an army for the next 15–20 years, and a commercial treaty was to be imposed on France making her economically dependent on Germany. Belgium, the document bluntly declares, 'must be reduced to a vassal state'. Luxemburg was to be annexed by the Reich. Holland was to be 'brought into closer relationship with the German Empire'. All these countries would join Germany and her allies Austria and Turkey – and perhaps also Italy, Sweden, Norway and Denmark and the new client states like Poland which were to be set up in western Russia – in a 'central European economic association' under German domination. This *Mitteleuropa* would have appended it to a *Mittelafrika*, a continous Central African colonial empire stretching from South-West Africa to Tanganyika and over into West Africa (Togo and the Cameroons), and thus including the Belgian Congo.

With the publication by Fischer of Bethmann Hollweg's 'September Programme' the cat was well and truly out of the bag – and if not among the pigeons then certainly among the hawks! The German historical establishment conspired frantically to silence Fischer and to discredit his work. They tried to exclude him from the archives, they withdrew funds for a lecture trip to America, they branded him a traitor and even a Soviet agent, they engaged in furious correspondence amongst themselves and with historian colleagues in other countries to try to convince them that Fischer was wrong – correspondence which was published, embarrassingly early, just a few years ago. But they were very short on arguments, and the pragmatically inclined French, British and American historical fraternity was in the end far more impressed by the archival material which Fischer had unearthed than by the allegedly suspect theories and concepts said by his opponents to underlie his heavily documented work. The Western historians were also repelled by the manifest unfairness of the treatment meted out to Fischer by his

German colleagues, which thus proved to be entirely counter-productive.

In the course of the 'Fischer controversy' which raged so furiously throughout the 1960s, Fischer's opponents concentrated on two things. First, they tried to rescue the figure of Chancellor Bethmann Hollweg from the wreckage. Though Bethmann Hollweg had composed and signed the 'September Programme', they argued that he must have done so under duress from the military, the Kaiser and his 'court clique', and sections of public opinion, so that the views expressed in the 'September Programme' were not really Bethmann's own. The quite irrational thinking which lay behind this rescue action to save Bethmann's reputation is revealed by the astonishing assertion of the German historian Michael Freund, writing in the prestigious *Frankfurter Allgemeine Zeitung* on 28 March 1964:

> If it turned out to be the case that in 1914 the same thing happened as in 1939, i.e. that there was a planned unleashing of a World War under the leadership of the German dictator [sic!], then we could finally shut the book of German history; then Hitler would always have ruled over us and would go on ruling over us for ever more.

Fischer effectively countered this argument by saying that his book was not about Bethmann's innermost feelings but about *German* policy, and that if Bethmann had indeed been forced against his better judgement to pursue expansionist aims, that only reinforced his, Fischer's, view that the forces of expansionism had become irresistible in Imperial Germany by 1914.

In my opinion this whole debate had in any case an air of unreality about it, since the office of Reich Chancellor had lost most of its independent decision-making power – particularly at the 'military-political' level – way back in the 1890s, in the long crisis which followed Bismarck's dismissal, so that by the time war broke out in 1914 the Chancellor and his civilian advisers are described in contemporary sources as sitting, isolated, in one corner of Imperial Military Headquarters, unable even to discover what the generals were up to, let alone influence their decisions. The debate was also unreal because practically nothing was known about Bethmann, all his Papers having been destroyed, it seems, when the Russians took over his family estate of Hohenfinow, north of Berlin, in 1945.

The second main thrust of Fischer's opponents in Germany was to try to represent the 'September Programme' not as the culmination of pre-war aspirations and as the aims to achieve which Germany had begun war in July 1914, but as an understandable reaction to the fact that Germany had found herself fighting not just against France and Russia but Great Britain as well. (They seemed only dimly aware that this position implied the admission that Germany had begun war deliberately against France and Russia.) But in any case the argument, tenuous at the best of times, came to lose all semblance of plausibility when it was later discovered that large segments of the 'September Programme' had been written down in the diary of Bethmann's assistant, a young man called Kurt Riezler, as early as mid-August 1914, i.e. within two or three weeks of the outbreak of war.

The crux of the controversy thus moved back in time to focus on the last two or three years of peace, the July crisis of 1914 itself, and the first few weeks of the war. Fischer set to work on a second book which eventually appeared in 1969 with the title *War of Illusions* and which established the continuity of German aims and policies from the Second Morocco Crisis of 1911 through to the September Programme of 1914. Meanwhile, his opponents were coming to realise that their arguments were proving quite ineffective against Fischer's documentary material, and that to make any impact they would have to discover documentary evidence of their own. This, however, proved more difficult than they anticipated.

The Riezler diary controversy

It is, in fact, remarkable how little evidence has survived regarding German intentions in the period 1909–14, compared with the years before and the years after that crucial period. The biggest loss of all was that of the Germany Army Archive, which was hit by an incendiary bomb and completely gutted in 1944. Some military papers that did survive the Second World War – such as those of General Erich Ludendorff – are even today closed to historical research. Other records have clearly been doctored or published in a falsified form. Just one example: Admiral von Müller was head of the Imperial Navy Cabinet from 1906 to 1918, and his diaries for the whole of that period have actually survived in manuscript form. They were published in 1965, and in this published version Müller is quoted as having written on 1 August 1914: 'In both [the Kaiser's and the Chancellor's] speeches the completely justified claim is made that we are the attacked.' But inspection of the original diary in the Military Archive in Freiburg reveals that Müller actually wrote: 'The mood is brilliant. The government has succeeded very well *in making us appear as the attacked.*' (My emphasis).

In these extraordinary circumstances it is not difficult to understand the excitement generated by the discovery that the diaries of Kurt Riezler, Bethmann Hollweg's personal assistant (1909–17), and the man who drafted part of the 'September Programme' had survived the Second World War (which Riezler, having a Jewish wife, had spent in the USA) and were, since Riezler's death in September 1955, in the hands of his brother in Munich. Surely this source would settle the argument one way or the other!

When the Fischer controversy broke in 1961, one of Fischer's bitterest opponents, the grand master of German historiography Professor Gerhard Ritter in Freiburg, wrote that the discovery of Kurt Riezler's diary was like an answer to a prayer; here would be the documentary proof that the traditionalists needed to show how wrong Fischer was to suggest that Bethmann Hollweg had wanted war in 1914. In March 1962 Ritter received a terrible shock from which he was never really to recover. A close colleague of his, Professor Hans Rothfels, who – being of Jewish origin – had like Riezler spent the war in America and had seen that volume of Riezler's diary covering the outbreak of war in July/August 1914, now warned Ritter that Riezler's diary, far from exonerating Bethmann, actually proved Fischer's interpretation is to be substantially correct. Bethmann's views, as recorded by Riezler, 'sounded as if *Bethmann Hollweg positively wanted war with Russia*', Rothfels informed him (My emphasis). Other people who had heard Riezler read from his diaries in New York similarly wrote of Bethmann Hollweg's *Kriegswilligkeit* – his will for war – in 1914; some even described the Chancellor as *kriegslustig*, as joyfully anticipating war. Rothfels actually admitted advising Riezler in 1945 or 1946 to destroy his diaries in the national interest.

In 1972 the eagerly-awaited publication of the Riezler diaries finally occurred. There was great excitement as pro-Fischerites and anti-Fischerites dissected the diary, each side claiming that the new evidence vindicated its position. And in the excitement only a couple of historians noticed that something was not quite in order. Several people who had read the diary for July 1914 had, as we have seen, gained the clear impression that Bethmann Hollweg was *kriegswillig, kriegslustig*, and 'positively wanted the war against Russia' during that fateful crisis. Now, the *published* diary entries for July 1914 showed a very different German Chancellor – a brooding, pessimistic, fatalistic philosopher musing about the inevitability of Russia's rise and Austria-Hungary's decline. Where, the sceptics now asked, was the evidence of his *Kriegswilligkeit*?

One of the few who in 1972 voiced his suspicion that everything was not as it should be was the young German historian Bernd Sösemann, then a mere *Assistent* at the University of Göttingen. For eight years he tried unsuccessfully to gain access to the manuscript Riezler diary which had been deposited in the Bundesarchiv in Koblenz when the edited version appeared. Finally, in 1980, permission was granted, and Sösemann discovered something that rocked the German historical establishment when his findings were published in 1983. What Sösemann discovered was that all the diary entries for the July Crisis of 1914, which the editor, Professor Karl Dietrich Erdmann of Kiel University, had declared to be the originals, were in fact quite different *in form* (and therefore possibly in content) from the rest of the diary. The scandal, when it broke, was enormous, and understandably so.

There is a second mystery surrounding the Riezler diaries, one which is potentially even more explosive than the first. Riezler began to keep a diary in 1907. Yet the first surviving exercise book is dated August 1914. This observation prompts a number of important but embarrassing questions:

- If the pre-war originals were not destroyed, where are they now?
- If they were destroyed, who destroyed them, when and why? Did the decision to burn them really have nothing to do with the Fischer controversy which broke out in 1961, only two years after the diaries are known to have been still intact?
- What happened to the transcripts Riezler's brother, Walter, was supposed to be making of the diaries?

The effect of the scandal over the Riezler diaries has been to cause much head-shaking in German historical circles. Most historians now agree that Fischer was basically right about German intentions in 1914, but instinctively – and perhaps understandably – they do not want to confront his awful truth. Often one hears them say privately that they can hardly bear to listen to any more about the July Crisis, Bethmann Hollweg and the September Programme. Their own research has tended to move away from that period and topic, and now concerns itself with social and organisational 'structures' on the one hand, and with abstractions such as the 'European states system' or the effect of Germany's central geographical position on her history on the other. Very few historians of any generation are now actively engaged on research into German policies in the 1911–14 period. And yet the debate must continue, for the riddle of 1914 has still not been solved.

1912 'War Council' controversy

One of the most intriguing documents to come to light in the course of the Fischer controversy over the origins of the First World War is Admiral von Müller's diary entry for 8 December 1912. Originally published in an adulterated form, it has been available in full since 1969, yet in all these years no one has really known quite what to make of it. There are those who rushed into print declaring the whole thing to be utterly insignificant – an odd reaction for scholars claiming to work in accordance with scientific and critical principles. At the other extreme there were historians – notably Adolf Gasser and Imanuel Geiss – who declared this to be the document which solved the whole mystery at a stroke: on Sunday, 8 December 1912, they said, the Kaiser and Germany's military leaders decided to begin a major European war in the summer of 1914, and everything that happened between the end of 1912 and August 1914 was in accord with that decision. In between were those who, more cautiously, suggested that the so-called 'war council' of 8 December 1912 was highly significant as a symptom of the state of mind of Germany's leaders, but that governments – and especially a government as chaotic and unstable as that of Imperial Germany – simply do not plan wars a year and a half in advance! For them, Müller's diary entry for 8 December 1912 was, in the literal sense, too good to be true.

Technically speaking there should be no problem here for the trained historian accustomed to evaluating historical evidence according to the established rules of his science. For the first point to bear in mind about Müller's diary entry for 8 December 1912 is that there is no doubt whatever about its authenticity – the diary has survived in its original handwritten version, and any scholar can inspect it in the Freiburg Military Archive. Secondly, the question of reliability of witness hardly arises, since Müller was one of the five or six people present at the meeting, and he set down his diary record of what had transpired at the conference later that same day. Thirdly, we now possess at least three other records of the meeting which, though they were composed at second or third hand, all broadly corroborate the Müller document.

According to the Admiral's diary for that Sunday morning, 8 December 1912, the Kaiser quite uncannily anticipated the sequence of events of July 1914. Wilhelm II was furious over a statement which Lord Haldane, speaking on behalf of Sir Edward Grey, had made a few days earlier to Prince Lichnowsky, the German ambassador in London, to the effect that if war were to break out in Europe, England would have to spring unconditionally to France's aid since it 'could not allow the balance of power in Europe to be disturbed'. At the hastily-convened meeting Kaiser Wilhelm declared:

Austria must deal energetically with the foreign Slavs (the Serbs), otherwise she will lose control of the Slavs in the Austro-Hungarian monarchy. If Russia supports the Serbs, which she evidently does (Sassonoff's declaration that Russia will immediately move into Galicia if Austria moves into Serbia) then war would be unavoidable for us too. We could hope, however, to have Bulgaria and Rumania and also Albania, and perhaps also Turkey on our side . . . If these powers join Austria then we shall be free to fight the war with full fury [*mit voller Wucht*] against France. The fleet must naturally prepare itself for the war against England. The possibility mentioned by the Chief of the Admiralty Staff in his last audience of a war with Russia alone cannot now, after Haldane's statement, be taken into account. Therefore immediate submarine warfare against English troop transports in the Scheldt or by Dunkirk, mine warfare in the Thames.

Turning to Admiral Tirpitz, the Kaiser recommended a 'speedy build-up of U-boats, etc.' and 'a conference of all interested naval authorities'. At this point, the Chief of the General Staff Helmuth von Moltke intervened. According to Müller he declared, already hinting, it seems, at the desirability of postponing the 'inevitable' war for a little while longer: 'I believe war is unavoidable. But we ought to do more through the press to prepare the popularity of a war against Russia, as suggested in the Kaiser's discussion.' It was Navy Secretary Tirpitz, however, who expressly demanded a '*postponement of the great fight for one-and-a-half years*', as Müller's diary records, thus giving that document its eerie significance. [My emphasis]. For of course a 'postponement of the great fight' against Britain, France and Russia for 18 months from December 1912 meant (if taken literally) 'unleashing' that war in the summer of 1914!

Admiral von Müller himself was a staunch advocate of immediate war, he favoured using the then current Balkan War and a cleverly drafted ultimatum as a convenient pretext to provoke war while making Russia seem the aggressor. His diary entry therefore ended on a note of disappointment:

That was the end of the conference. The result amounted to almost nothing. The Chief of the Great General Staff says: War the sooner the better, but he does not draw the logical conclusion from this, which is: To present Russia or France or both with an ultimatum which would *unleash the war with right on our side*. [My emphasis]

On the morning of Monday, 9 December 1912, Captain Albert Hopman of the Imperial Navy Office heard from his masseur (!) that there had been a meeting of Germany's highest-ranking Army and Navy leaders in the Kaiser's Schloss on the previous day. Hopman learned later from Tirpitz (as he recorded in his diary) that the Kaiser had summoned the meeting because Lichnowsky had reported from London that Haldane had declared:

> If a general European war should break out, England would stand on France's side, since it could not tolerate that any one Power should gain a position of pronounced predominance on the Continent. His Majesty [Tirpitz went on] therefore regarded the situation as very grave, especially as Sasonow is supposed to have said that if Austria attacked Serbia, Russia would hit out. His Majesty sees Austria's demands as expressing the vital interests of the Habsburg Monarchy which she can on no account give up and which we [Germany] must support. [He] does not believe that Serbia will knuckle under. The Chief of the General Staff regards war as unavoidable and says the sooner the better. Tirpitz contradicted him and said it lay in the interest of the Navy *to postpone war if possible for 1–2 years* [My emphasis]. The Army, too, could do much in the intervening time to make better use of our surplus population.

As time goes by, more and more evidence is coming to light in regard to this extraordinary meeting and its aftermath. The British historian, Terence F. Cole, has recently unearthed in the Berne archives a copy – significantly the original has disappeared – of a fascinating report compiled on 10 December 1912 by the veteran Swiss ambassador in Berlin, de Claparède, of a conversation he had on that day with the Kaiser. In it, the ambassador describes the Kaiser's 'grave and agitated' tirade at recent developments in the Balkans and the consequences these would have for German policy. The war of the Balkan States against Turkey was, the monarch had said, 'not a religious war but purely a racial war, the war of Slavdom against Germandom'. Russia, who stood behind the Balkan League, clearly intended 'to unite all Slavs, not merely those of the Balkans, but the Slavs of other States, in particular of Austria-Hungary, so weakening Austria militarily through the loss of so-and-so million Slavs.' Austria, however, was fully aware of the danger 'and we in Germany too, and we will not leave our Ally in the lurch: if diplomacy fails, we shall have to fight this racial war'. Only a few days earlier, the Kaiser told Claparède, he had learnt that Lord Haldane had announced to Lichnowsky 'that England would never tolerate Germany's taking a predominant position over her neighbours in Central Europe. Is this not an impertinent statement which should really have been answered by a breaking off of diplomatic relations?', the Kaiser demanded indignantly, 'Is it not incredible . . . that these Anglo-Saxons with whom we are related by common ancestry, religion and civilisatory striving, now wish to allow themselves to be used as tools of the Slavs,' Wilhelm exclaimed. The Kaiser then declared that Austria and Germany would have to prevent the creation of a strong Serbian State. The vital interests of both empires required that they must not be 'encircled by a Slav ring'. Again he stated emphatically:

> If this question . . . cannot be solved by diplomacy, then it will have to be decided by armed force. The solution can be postponed [echoing the 'decision' of the 'war council' of two days earlier]. But the question will arise again in 1 or 2 years . . . *The racial struggle cannot be avoided – perhaps it will not take place now, but it will probably take place in one or two years.* [My emphasis]

One of the participants of this 'military political conference' (this is what Müller called it – Bethmann Hollweg referred to the meeting more bitterly as a 'war council') in the Kaiser's Schloss was Vice-Admiral von Heeringen, whose brother was the Prussian War Minister. It was from the latter that the Saxon and Bavarian military plenipotentiaries in Berlin learned further details of the conference of 8 December 1912. According to the report of the meeting sent to Dresden by General von Leuckart, Saxony's military envoy, General von Moltke had declared he

> wants war because he believes that it would not now be welcome to France, as is shown by the fact of her intervention in support of a peaceful solution to the situation. His Excellency v. *Tirpitz on the other hand would prefer it if it [i.e. war] came in one year's time, when the [Kiel] Canal and the harbour for submarines in Heligoland would be ready.* [My emphasis]

The Bavarian military plenipotentiary, General von Wenninger, reported even more fully on the conference of the top Army and Navy leaders that the Kaiser had convened on the previous Sunday. On 15 December 1912, he wrote to his superiors in Munich:

> A week ago today H.M. summoned Moltke, Tirpitz and Müller (Bethmann [Hollweg], [War Minister] Heeringen and Kiderlen [the Foreign Secretary] were not invited!) and informed them in a most agitated state that he had heard from Lichnowsky that Haldane had come to tell him, probably on Grey's orders, 'England would stand on the side of Germany's enemies, whether Germany attacked or was herself attacked [. . .]. England could not look on while France was thrown completely to the ground and a Power arose on the Continent which possessed absolute hegemony in Europe.' Moltke wanted to launch an immediate

attack; there had not been a more favourable opportunity since the formation of the Triple Alliance. *Tirpitz demanded a postponement for one year, until the [Kiel] Canal and the U-Boat harbour on Heligoland were finished. The Kaiser agreed to a postponement only reluctantly* [My emphasis]. He told the War Minister the following day only that he should prepare a new large Army Bill immediately. Tirpitz received the same order for the Fleet. The War Minister likewise demanded the postponement of the introduction of the Bill until the autumn . . . The War Minister told me this himself . . . The Kaiser ordered the General Staff and the Admiralty Staff to work out an invasion of England in grand style. Meanwhile his diplomats are to seek allies everywhere, Rumania (already partly secured), Bulgaria, Turkey etc. Your Excellency will see that the picture behind the scenes is very different from that on the official stage.

It will be granted that all five of these records – Müller's, Hopman's, Leuckart's, Wenninger's and Claparède's – corroborate one another to a quite exceptional degree. In each, the same points are made, sometimes with almost identical wording, sometimes with significant variation. It is fascinating to have Hopman's account of his conversation with Tirpitz, for example, because Tirpitz there confirmed – on the day *after* the 'war council' – his conviction that a great war should be 'postponed'; but Hopman quotes him as using the more flexible formula 'if possible for one to two years' rather than Müller's precise 'one-and-a-half years'. The recently-discovered Swiss ambassador's report of his conversation with Wilhelm II on 10 December 1912 is of such interest because, though it does not refer to the military-political meeting of 8 December 1912, it does show that Kaiser Wilhelm II had accepted and internalised Tirpitz's 'window of opportunity' notion that the great 'racial' war against 'Slavdom', the 'Gauls' and the 'Anglo-Saxons' should be fought not immediately but in one or two years' time. The widening of the Kiel Canal to accommodate the new Dreadnoughts, to which two of the reports refer, was in fact completed in late June 1914, just a few days before the assassination of the Archduke Franz Ferdinand and his wife at Sarajevo in Austrian Bosnia on 28 June.

Some conclusions

I would very much like to know what readers of these documents make of them. Fresh ideas from younger, more flexible minds might help to solve a riddle which has foxed professional historians for three-quarters of a century. What is needed, in particular, are suggestions as to how the hypothesis that the German leaders in December 1912 'postponed' a great war against Britain, France and Russia for one to two years – which is what the documents seem to indicate clearly enough – might be either verified or falsified. Of course if Riezler's diary were available for the period 1912–14, the answer would presumably be a matter of record, one way or the other!

To me personally, as research into these issues progresses, the conclusion seems more and more inescapable that at the end of the nineteenth century, Imperial Germany under Kaiser Wilhelm II embarked on a long-term bid to secure 'world power' status by using Tirpitz's battlefleet plan as a lever to effect a revolutionary shift in the global balance of power in Germany's favour. By prising Great Britain out of her position as guarantor of the balance of power in Europe, the Continent would come under German domination, it was calculated, with or without a war. Germany would then be able to expand without hindrance into the Middle East. Once the Royal Navy no longer blocked her way, only the United States of America would be able to oppose German domination of Latin America south of the Amazon, and only the Japanese Empire would stand in her way in China. By about 1909, however, it was becoming clear that this gigantic 'bid for world power' was failing. The British were outbuilding and outmanoeuvring Tirpitz at sea, the Triple Entente had been formed to 'contain', 'encircle' or 'isolate' Germany internationally, and the tide of democracy and socialism at home was threatening to sweep away the very pillars on which the Prusso-German military monarchy was based. Most menacing of all, the multi-national Austro-Hungarian Empire, the German Reich's only serious ally, was in a state of rapid and terminal decline.

In this situation Germany's hopelessly irrational governmental system, in which the Kaiser, his Court and above all his Generals played a bigger role than the civilian Chancellor and his civilian Foreign Secretary, opted for what they called 'preventive war' (in objective terms it was in fact an offensive war of expansion) as the tried and tested Prussian solution to both the foreign and domestic *impasse* that had been reached. For more than two decades the Great General Staff had been elaborating, practising and perfecting the Schlieffen Plan. The Railway Department of the General Staff had divided Germany into 3,000 segments, in each of which mobility was constantly being improved through the building of new tracks and bridges. As 1914 approached, the Schlieffen Plan envisaged the clockwork mobilisation of 3.8 million men and their deployment over a war zone of 275,000 square miles. In the first 12 days of the Plan, 60,000 railway carriages full of men, 105,000 carriages full of horses and 59,000 carriages of weapons and supplies had to reach the Western Front: 590 trains per day would have to thunder over the Rhine bridges during this first phase of hostilities. The entire war against first France and then Russia was planned to last precisely 70 days. In the Spring of 1913, when the decision had already been taken to increase the size of the German Army by one third, forcing France with its much smaller and older population to increase its military service to three years, with chaotic consequences, Germany's *Ostaufmarschplan*, which envisaged the Eastern Front as the main theatre of warfare, was declared defunct: the Schlieffen Plan was henceforth, by choice, the only military plan available to the German General Staff. My point is that, given such precision planning over decades, such reliance on split-second timing to move several million men, the question of *how* and *when* this immense war machine should be set in motion cannot have been a matter of indifference to the German Generals.

So great was the faith in the Generals and their Plan that the civilian statesmen did not feel impelled to seek a political or diplomatic solution to Germany's grave problems at home and abroad. Her military and civilian leaders appear to have agreed that in starting a war they had to make it *seem* as if Russia were the aggressor, and that a Balkan crisis involving Austria – perhaps coupled with an ultimatum to 'unleash the war with right on our side' – was the best way to achieve that. Virtually the only issue dividing them was that of timing. From 1911 to 1914 the German leadership (and this includes Chancellor von Bethmann Hollweg) appears no longer to have been asking how war against the three Entente Powers could be avoided, but only: When will we be ready? When will the other side begin to catch up? When is the best time for us to 'go', to 'strike', '*loszuschlagen*'? What can we do in the interval to improve our chances? How can we, when the time comes, provoke war while '*making us appear as the attacked*?

On the last day of 1911, the Crown Prince wrote to his father the Kaiser that 'as a result of quiet and careful reflection' he was hoping that the new year (1912) would bring war, a *Waffengang*:

> The German nation [he wrote] has reached a turning point, it will either rise or fall. The well-known Place in the Sun has not been accorded to us, and so we shall have to gain it by force of arms. At the same time I have concluded that the confused and hopeless domestic situation would improve at a stroke if all the people of our country were called upon to take up arms, and I am convinced that the rest of the world will stare in shock and wonder at the sight of an awakened strong Germany determined to fight to the finish.

In the event, 'Little Willie' had to wait a little longer for his *Waffengang*. On 30 July 1914 Rudolf von Valentini, the head of the Kaiser's Civil Cabinet, was invited to dine at the New Palace in Potsdam, where he met the Kaiser, the Crown Prince and the other Imperial Princes. 'All,' he recorded in his diary, were 'full of *Kriegslust*'.

Further Reading

Berghahn, V.R. *Germany and the Approach of War in 1914* (London, 1973).

Bucholz, A. *Schlieffen and Prussian War Planning* (Oxford, 1990).

Evans, R.J.W. and Pogge von Strandmann, H. (eds) *The Coming of the First World War* (Oxford, 1988).

Fischer, F. *Germany's Aims in the First World War* (London, 1967).

Fischer, F. *War of Illusions* (London, 1975).

Geiss, I. *July 1914: Selected Documents* (London, 1972).

Geiss, I. *German Foreign Policy 1871–1914* (London, 1976).

Joll, J. *The Origins of the First World War* (London and New York, 1984).

John Röhl is the author of several books on Imperial Germany. He is Professor of History at the University of Sussex.

Peter Catterall
Examiner's Report

Peter Catterall dissects a student essay illustrating many of the problems and pitfalls students encounter when trying to write about modern European history.

Question

To what extent was the Paris Commune relevant to the development of the socialist movement?

Student's answer by 'Emily'

In March 1871 popular insurrection broke out in Paris. The Parisians had been provoked into action by the months of hardship they had endured whilst under siege by the Prussian army. The rebels were also taking a stand against the French government in Versailles as they did not agree with the government's handling of the situation. The insurrection was finally repressed in May 1871 and immediately became a legendary episode eventually becoming known as the Commune. Trying to establish its relevance to the socialist movement is not easy when on the one hand Marx wrote two days after the end of the Commune on May 30, 1871:

> Working-mens's Paris, with the Commune, will be forever celebrated as the glorious harbinger of a new society. Its martyrs are enshrined in the great heart of the working class.

On the other hand, Alfred Cobban, the distinguished historian of France, writes:

> It is a mistake to regard the Commune as Marxist in inspiration . . . Equally it was not a government of the working class.

The introduction to an essay should locate the subject and establish the issues to be explored. Emily has successfully done the latter here, and her two quotes neatly juxtapose different responses to the Commune. She should, however, have noted that, in terms of exploring the relevance of the Commune to the subsequent history of the Left the reaction of Marx — himself, of course, the most distinguished and influential contemporary would-be revolutionary – is far more significant than that of a twentieth century British historian.

She could also have done much more to locate the circumstances of the Commune. We are told nothing of the context of the Prussian siege, the harsh peace terms demanded and the political divisions which they opened up in France over peace or war, Republic or Monarchy. Nor are we told of the way German pressure led Thiers to resolve forcibly to remove cannon from Paris, which precipitated the events of 18 March 1871 and the establishment of Communal control of the city. The consequence is that the ensuing discussion of the Commune is not rooted in any hard facts about the factors which brought it about or the circumstances it confronted.

The Paris Commune came in the second half of a century punctuated by popular revolt. Therefore for European rulers, industrialists and conservatives, the Commune confirmed the fear of an international revolutionary movement with, possibly, the imminent danger of a socialist revolution in their own country. The Commune also re-instated their fear that the International Working-Men's Association (First International) was really a staff for universal revolution. Meanwhile the revolutionaries in Europe saw the Commune as yet another failed revolution. At the same time, it emphasised, to those interested, that revolutionaries should revise their methods. After all, it seemed to prove the failure of old-style urban insurrections.

It is impossible to deny that the Commune was a great influence upon Karl Marx and the First International. Just before the Commune, the purpose of the International was wavering. There was a schism amongst its members, between those who followed Marx and those who followed Bakunin. The Commune gave the International a popular significance greater than it had had in its own lifetime. The International declared the Commune as its own inspiration and Marx declared in his address of May 30, 1871:

It is but natural that members of our Association shall stand in the foreground . . . wherever . . . the class struggle obtains any consistency.

Emily is right to draw attention to the fear of revolution in nineteenth century Europe. But how grave a threat was posed either by the First International or the Commune? On the face of it, the situation the government faced in Paris was potentially no less threatening than for its predecessors in 1830 and 1848. The new republican government which had succeeded to power upon the military defeat of Napoleon III's Second Empire was, in fact in many ways, in no stronger a position than the monarchical regimes overthrown on those previous occasions. There was limited support for the new regime even amongst the political élite, and the newly elected Assembly, which met for the first time on 20 March, had a conservative, royalist majority. Concerns about the risk of a royalist coup d'état were, in fact, a factor in the dissatisfaction that fuelled the rising. Another factor was concern amongst the bellicose Parisians, having endured a long Prussian siege, at the peace terms that might be accepted by the assembly which had been elected to negotiate them.

The assembly would at least support the government against 'the mob'. Whether the army would as well was initially much less clear. The troops in Paris were also, as in 1830 and 1848, too few to deal effectively with the insurrectionists, prompting a prudent government to withdraw them to Versailles. Its difficulties were then swiftly compounded by further risings over the following week in Lyons, Marseilles, Narbonne, St Etienne and Le Creusot.

The government, nevertheless, was not immediately threatened. It was not located in Paris and vulnerable to the volatile politics of the capital. Instead it was initially in Bordeaux, moving to Versailles, some ten miles from Paris, in March. This, and the military withdrawal, enabled the government to regroup and work to improve the discipline and morale of its troops. The army's initial reaction, meanwhile, lulled the Parisians into over-confidence that a conscript army would swiftly desert to them once they marched on Versailles. This was to prove a fatal error on the part of the Communards. The government, although at first put on the defensive, retained the means to suppress the rising, and this proved decisive. The Commune was defeated militarily after a hard-fought and bloody struggle. In this sense Emily is right to see the Commune as the last of the old-style urban insurrections, and a sign that these were no longer so likely to succeed. This is a good point, but it is not fully developed or supported here. It might also be better to keep a point like this for the conclusion, where it could be used to suggest that the Commune perhaps marked the end of one type of revolutionary activity, rather than a stage in the development of the socialist movement.

Instead it is thrown in here rather awkwardly. The subsequent shift to talking about Marx and the International is rather a non sequitur (an abrupt change of subject which does not really fit with the preceding argument). Here, again, Emily oversimplifies. She neglected to mention that the International, quite apart from the in-fighting between anarchists and Marxists, also contained an admixture of English reformist trade unionists, many of whom would not have seen the Parisian revolutionary tradition as the way forward. Some of these, like George Odger, could not stomach Marx's glorification of the Commune and resigned. Differences in their interpretation of the Commune meanwhile exacerbated the existing conflict between Marx and Bakunin, and contributed to the latter's expulsion from the International in 1872. By 1876, just five years after the Commune, the organisation itself had been wound up. The Commune was initially a threat to the political order in France. The International was much less formidable.

Marx hesitated slightly at the time before giving his opinion about the Commune. However, once he had decided it was significant to the socialist movement, he was swift to show the relevance. For example, he talks about 'Paris armed was the Revolution armed'. He also claimed that the Commune was essentially a working-class government, the product of the struggle of the producing against the appropriating class, the political form, at last discovered, under which to work out the economic emancipation of labour.

It is possible to argue that Marx exaggerates the socialist aspect or ideals of the Commune when he talks about the Commune's intention to abolish property.

Non-Marxist socialists, such as M Wincock and J P Azéma, differ from Marx in not seeing the Communal government as a 'worker regime resolved to overturn a capitalist regime'. But as socialists they do see the Commune as the first revolutionaries of the industrial age, expressing the hope for a radically new world and the Commune as one of the greatest events in labour history. They argue that it is not possible to 'discern in the Communal movement any conscious or systematic desire to destroy capitalism'. They further dispute with Marx, saying that the Commune's 'hesitations' only go to show its lack of class consciousness.

One of the effects of the French Revolution that began in 1789 was the idea that the sudden and dramatic overthrow of the existing order was possible and the division of much of Europe's political classes into those who feared this and those professional revolutionaries who desired to bring it about. Karl Marx was one of the latter. He saw in the Commune, as his The Civil War in France *makes clear, the revolution he expected. For Marx did not just hope for a revolution and theorise about it. He predicted it. But the revolution he anticipated was not simply a political revolution against an* ancien regime. *Schooled by his friend, Friedrich Engels' observations of the effects of industrialisation in Britain, particularly in* The Condition of the Working Class in England *published in 1844, he expected an increasingly exploitative monopoly capitalism to prompt a working-class revolution. Indeed, he explained all history in terms of such conflicts over economic modes of production. In this case a revolution by the working classes against their bourgeois exploiters was not just desirable, but inevitable. The episode of the Commune was easily slotted into this theory of class conflict. Marx, indeed, celebrated what he saw as the Commune's intention*

> *to abolish that class-property which makes the labour of many the wealth of the few. It aimed at the expropriation of the expropriators.*

This was of course exactly what Marx anticipated the revolution should entail.

All this raises two important questions. The first of these, as Emily is aware, is whether or not Marx's reading of the Commune is correct. She has juxtaposed some different views. But she conveys them in a confused way. She relies too heavily on rather repetitious quotes from Wincock and Azéma, and tells us nothing about the hopes and aspirations of the Commune itself. She presents no evidence here from which we can judge whether or not the Commune was a Marxist revolution. The voting in Paris in the February elections suggests that the capital was solidly Republican, the heroes and exiles of 1848 heading the poll, but not revolutionary. Indeed, would-be revolutionaries, such as Auguste Blanqui, trailed far behind.

Following the shock of the election of a monarchist assembly and the subsequent confrontation of 18 March the pendulum swung to the left, but there were still 21 anti-Communards elected in the polls that led to the establishment of the Commune on 28 March. If the rest constituted Marx's predicted 'dictatorship of the proletariat', it was a distinctly middle class one.

The Commune certainly involved the occupation of workshops and factories abandoned by the middle classes. But the rhetoric was as much about safeguarding the Republic in the face of the assembly, as of building the revolution. Marx might have been clear about what he thought the Commune should have stood for, and in his writings he painted the Commune in his image. At the time the Commune was much clearer as to what it stood against.

This raises a second important question. It is clear that the Commune inspired Marx, who spoke of the Communards 'storming heaven'. But did it have any effect on the development of his views? This is an important issue in this essay, but it is one Emily does not address. If the Commune merely confirmed Marx in his views it cannot be said to have played a major part in the development of the socialist movement. Certainly it does not seem to have contributed significantly to the theoretical adaptations of the last years of his life, such as accepting, that Britain might undergo the hoped-for transformation without needing a revolution. What was important was the idea of the seizure of power. For future revolutionaries, tutored by Marx's writings, the Commune was the model of how to achieve their ends. Lenin based his State and Revolution, *written whilst awaiting his opportunity in 1917, on* The Civil War in France. *The Bolsheviks consciously counted the days during their first weeks in power, until they had surpassed the Commune as the longest-surviving 'Communist' regime. It was through this image of the Commune, mediated and to some extent manufactured by Marx, that it was to have its most enduring legacy. There were, however, other interpretations, to which Emily now turns.*

Following the insurrection, the Daru Committee was set up to look at the origins of the insurrection of March 18. The Committee submitted its report to the assembly on 22 December 1871. It illustrated the essentially conservative attitudes of the old liberal position. The report calls the insurrection a 'new invasion of barbarians', who 'do not so much wish to destroy the city of stone as the city of morality'. The report claims that the Commune 'has just shown insane theories at work, false programmes whose realisation would set humanity back several centuries.' As for socialism, the contemporary novelist Flaubert wrote, 'it will be dead for a long time'.

Quotes, such as those cited here, can suggest a superficial familiarity with the subject and the historiographical literature. However, Emily's essay, here and elsewhere comes dangerously close to being an anthology of quotes, rather than an essay which uses these effectively to support her argument. She does not explain the attitudes which lie behind the quotes.

Nor does she get to grips with some of the difficult concepts she uses here. A familiar problem in students' essays is a tendency to use words such as 'conservatism' or 'socialism' without any indication as to what the student thinks they mean. This is a trap Emily has fallen into here. In particular, without some explanation as to what she means by 'conservative' and 'liberal', her comment about 'the essentially conservative attitudes of the old liberal position' is meaningless. People like Daru were liberals under the previous regime. He had been an opponent of Napoleon III, but had agreed to serve in his Liberal Empire in January 1870. The political situation in 1871 was, however, completely different. Emily would have done herself, and her readers, a lot of favours if she had tried to explain more of the complex politics of France 1870–71 at an early point in her essay. It is only now that she begins to consider this.

Within the Commune there were the pure revolutionaries, who were divided between the Blanquists and the Jacobins, the federalists following Proudhon and the Marxist adherents of the First International. Therefore it would appear that Marx's claim for a strong connection between the Commune and the First International is ill-founded, especially in view of the fact that few of the leaders of the Commune were more than loosely connected with the Commune.

This passage does not get us much further, because Emily does not explain who the various groups are that she refers to, or the differences of opinion between them. Neither the Jacobins, who looked back to the heroic days of 1793, or the Blanquists, could properly be termed socialists. Blanqui, indeed, was contemptuous of socialism and boycotted the International's congresses. His idea of a dedicated revolutionary élite was nevertheless to be influential on later socialists, finding its way into Russian revolutionary thought through his contributions to their journals at the end of his long life in the 1880s. This idea was perhaps another legacy of the Commune to later revolutionaries such as Lenin.

The followers of Proudhon were socialists, but of a very different stamp from Marx. In a France where industry remained largely small-scale he advocated not the abolition of property, but its redistribution. Capitalism would be replaced by mutual relations between a federation of self-governing units, or Communes. *These ideas, which were sufficiently important for Marx to devote a book* (The Poverty of Philosophy) *to attacking them, seem to have been more influential in shaping the Commune than those of Marx or the First International. The significance of the latter was, however, far from negligible. Of the 92 delegates elected to the Commune, 17 were representatives of the International, compared to 9 Blanquists. In these circumstances Emily seems to be overly dismissive of its role.*

I would argue that the Commune never posed a real threat to any European country and, in fact, the period from March to May 1871 was of little relevance to the development of the socialist movement. I think it would be true to say that at the time the European governments and authorities perceived the Commune as a serious threat. This was partly due to the atmosphere at the time. It was also seen as a threat simply because of its name. For many, especially in France, this brought back painful memories of year II of the Revolution, of the Jacobins, of Robespierre and the *sans-culottes*. The word 'commune' also contained anti-capitalist connotations.

However, in my opinion, the Paris Commune has been forced into influencing the development of the socialist movement through the works of one man, Karl Marx. Through his distorted interpretation, the Commune appeared to be extremely relevant to the development of the socialist movement. Lenin said that, 'the young Soviet Republic stood on the shoulders of the Paris Commune'. This reflects the importance of the Marxian interpretation of the Commune for Soviet ideology.

I think most people would find it extremely hard to dispute the fact that Marx has been one of the greatest influences on the socialist movement. It was Marx who took the events of 1871 and turned them into such an important development for the socialist movement. In summary, the Paris Commune was and still is very relevant to the development of the socialist movement, not because of what happened, but because of what Karl Marx believed happened.

It is always a good idea to end your essays, if possible, with a strong sentence which underlines the argument pursued. Emily's final sentence is a good example of this, bringing her essay to a very effective end.

However, her final three paragraphs continue to suffer from structural and stylistic flaws. This is particularly true of the first paragraph. She would have been better advised to reverse the order in which she placed her points so as to improve the flow of the argument and establish more effectively the contrast with which she begins the following paragraph.

It would also improve the flow of her argument if she avoided repetition. This can give a rather stilted feel to an essay. It is not necessary to keep on repeating the terms of the question, to show that you remember it. She could at least have varied it by referring to the 'growth of socialism' as an alternative on occasion. Showing a broader range of linguistic skills cannot do any harm and will help to maintain the interest and engage the sympathies of the examiners.

Emily would also be well-advised to avoid the use of phrases such as 'I think' or 'in my opinion'. In so far as the essay is necessarily her opinion anyway, such phrases are of course utterly redundant. But of course history essays are not just exercises in expressing personal opinions. They should also be based, to a greater extent than this one is, on the deployment of evidence. The argument should be rooted in this evidence, not based on opinion. If you feel a need to make specific references to help move the argument along, you should refer to this evidence, and not to 'my opinion'. So, when you next feel tempted to put 'I think' in a history essay, consider the merits of using a phrase such as 'in the light of the evidence cited' instead.

Unfortunately, there is far too little evidence cited in this particular essay. Emily's discussion of the Paris Commune operates almost entirely out of context. Writing a history essay which consisted entirely of evidence and no argument would obviously be wrong. But the various points in your argument do need to be supported by evidence. You also need to show that you have properly considered the evidence, and are not just selecting the bits which suit you. Emily's essay falls short on these criteria. After all, it is crucial to her concluding remarks that the reader agrees that she has established that Marx's view of the Commune was distorted. Unfortunately, she never tells us enough about the Commune to support this point.

Peter Catterall is Director of the Institute of Contemporary British History, Visiting Lecturer in History at Queen Mary and Westfield College, London and Editor of *Modern History Review*.

Index